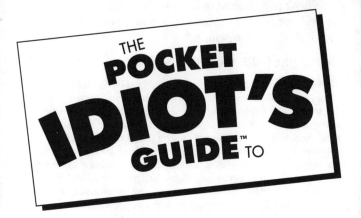

Golf Accessories

by Rich Mintzer

alpha
books

A Division of Macmillan General Reference
A Pearson Education Macmillan Company
1633 Broadway, New York, NY 10019-6785

This book is dedicated to Eric and Rebecca, future golfers; as well as to everyone who's ever said "It can't be my game, it must be my clubs."

Copyright © 1999 by Rich Mintzer

Macmillan Publishing books may be purchased for business or sales promotional use. For information please write: Special Markets Department, Macmillan Publishing USA, 1633 Broadway, New York, NY 10019.

International Standard Book Number: 0-02-863376-8
Library of Congress Catalog Card Number available upon request.

02   01   00   99   4   3   2   1

Interpretation of the printing code: the rightmost number of the first series of numbers is the year of the book's printing; the rightmost number of the second series of numbers is the number of the book's printing. For example, a printing code of 99-1 shows that the first printing occurred in 1999.

Printed in the United States of America

Contents

Introduction

Golf is a game rich in history and tradition. It's a game like no other and often is considered to be a way of life for the avid player. As in all sports, there's a need for the right equipment. Through centuries of trial and error and modern technology, equipment has become scientifically calculated to perform at the highest levels. There's an ongoing quest in the golf world to create better clubs, balls that travel farther, and lighter bags. The following are some improvements:

- Club and ball design has become a combination of art and science. It utilizes computers and a variety of testing devices combined with designers' careful blueprints. New metals are tested to be potentially used in clubs, and a wide variety of materials are used on both the inside and outside of the golf ball. To maintain the integrity of the game, balls and clubs must conform to a list of guidelines set forth by golf's governing body, the United States Golf Association.

- Golf glove, shoe, and bag manufacturers try to find the perfect combination of materials for comfort and durability on the golf course.

- Clothing manufacturers also work hard to create loose-fitting, comfortable attire in a variety of styles and price ranges, to wear on the course and look fashionable while playing.

The right equipment and clothing can also build a player's confidence. If you look good and believe you can hit a certain brand of ball farther with a club you feel is designed for your game, you'll often fare much better. As most golfers will tell you, more than half of this great game is mental.

Variations on a Theme

What makes golf more distinctive than other sports is the endless variations of the playing field. Although the rules are the same, no two golf courses in the world are identical—not even the few that specifically try to duplicate classic courses.

This book is designed to give you a basic overview of the wealth of equipment and accessories on the market today. Even as you read, however, you can be sure that, in this modern technological age, someone is diligently creating a new ball with yet another dimple pattern (of which there have been thousands) or a golf bag that practically hovers behind you so you need not carry it.

What Do I Really Need to Play This Game?

Some ability is first on the list, meaning a basic degree or level of skill to hit the ball. Next comes the all-important level of confidence. Beyond that, it varies greatly. You might have heard of some skilled golfer who, either after losing a bet or on a dare, played an 18-hole course using just one ball and a 3-iron. You also might have seen people set out on the course with a huge golf bag stuffed with everything imaginable from a complete set of clubs to a portable TV and mini refrigerator. Chances are, you'll land somewhere in between in your preparedness to play.

You probably will want the following:

- Balls, clubs, and a bag are your three most basic needs.

- Tees are small and inexpensive yet very important.

- Golf shoes provide better footing on a variety of (often damp) course surfaces and help keep your feet in place while you swing the club.

- Golf gloves, while certainly not mandatory, can help you find a surer grip on the club and can prevent the discomfort that comes from hitting the ball on a cool day.

From here, it's up to you. A towel can keep your hands clean, a repair kit can make fixing divots easier, pencils can help you keep score if you choose to, and so on. The sport is booming, and a wealth of products are available. You'll choose what you need based on your devotion to the game.

This book gives you the lowdown on buying balls, clubs, bags, shoes, and other accessories. You need not take everything into consideration, just as you don't consider every option available when buying a new car. Just consider what's important to you. Nonetheless, as your enthusiasm for the game grows—and it will—you might want to look back and be a more savvy shopper when you buy your second pair of golf shoes or when you replace a few of your irons with fairway woods.

Equipment continues to improve with the advent of new technology. As your game improves, you'll want to upgrade your tools as well. Do not make the mistake, however, of overemphasizing your equipment at the expense of improving your skills. Despite claims by manufacturers regarding balls that travel farther and clubs that will have you hitting longer and straighter, more golfers lower their handicap with lessons and frequent visits to the practice range than by constantly buying new equipment.

Ultimately, what you need is equipment that suits you and your game. As great as Tiger Woods and the PGA and LPGA players are, what works for them will not necessarily work for you. Look at the features of the particular ball, club, or shoes and see whether they'll be beneficial to your needs.

It also is worth mentioning that you need not buy the first club that feels good in your hand. Shopping around is part of the fun. Most major cities have annual or twice-annual golf shows at their convention centers. Many major golf manufacturers set up demo days in which they come to your town and let you try out their latest line of equipment at the golf course. The 800 numbers in the back of this book serve as a resource for reaching the manufacturers' catalogs or to find out when a demo day will take place in your area. Finally, retail outlets and pro shops have clubs, bags, and various equipment right there for you to check out.

Where Do I Shop?

Nearly every course in the world has a pro shop or golf shop, which can range in size, scope, and inventory. An upscale course often has an upscale pro shop. An inexpensive municipal course might have just a small shop with a limited inventory. Either way, you often can find some of the name brands you are looking for. Some pro shops will offer used clubs being sold for good prices. It's important that such clubs are comfortable and in good shape. Ask if you can hit a few shots at the range or in the practice facility to try them out.

In addition to pro shops, sporting goods stores carry golf equipment, and local individually owned golf shops can be found sprinkled throughout major cities. Larger golf retailers also have cropped up in recent years. Like all other big things in America, golf is beginning to see superstores emerging. Last, but certainly not least, is the tremendous catalog business. Shopping at home via catalogs and the Internet is big business, and golf is certainly a part of that.

Four of the biggest golf retail chains and catalog distributors are described in the following sections.

Edwin Watts Golf Shops

Edwin Watts is a 47-store chain founded by none other than Edwin Watts. From a single pro shop in 1968, this retail business grew quickly throughout the southern part of the United States. Led by 21 stores in Florida, the chain now occupies nearly one million square feet of space containing golf equipment and accessories. The stores carry all the major brands and sell golf essentials at competitive prices. You also can be custom-fitted with top-of-the-line golf equipment. Some of the superstores even display antique clubs and golf memorabilia. To satisfy the rest of the country and to reach out to customers worldwide, there also is a massive mail-order business with five separate seasonal catalogs distributed each year. Edwin Watts can be reached at 1-800-874-0146 (or for international customers, 1-850-244-2066) or **www.edwinwatts.com.**

Golf Day

During the past 20 years, Golf Day has evolved from a small inauspicious start in the early 1970s to a major retail operation in the 1990s. In the past 10 years, the company has grown by leaps and bounds into one of a few major players specifically dealing in golf retail. Now sporting 84 shops throughout the northeast plus four stores in southern California, Golf Day is one of the premiere locations for East Coast golfers to find their clubs, balls, bags, and so on. Carrying all the top name brands, Golf Day puts out a catalog four times a year detailing their vast inventory. To find a nearby location or to get a catalog, their toll-free number is 1-800-676-4653 or visit their Web site at **www.golfday.com.**

Golfsmith

Golfsmith International was founded as a golf club components industry in 1967. It since has expanded to offer golf equipment and accessories through catalogs and retail superstores.

The 24 superstores are located in Texas, Colorado, Illinois, New York, New Jersey, Minnesota, Ohio, Pennsylvania, Washington, Georgia, Arizona, and California as well as in Canada. Stores primarily are in the 20,000 to 30,000 square feet range and are stocked with a huge inventory of golf equipment, apparel, gift items, accessories, and more. Golfsmith carries all the leading brand names. Also featured at Golfsmith superstores are items such as an indoor waterfall and putting green, computerized swing analyzers, and huge video walls tuned to golf programming.

The components and store catalogs have a combined circulation of 32 million and can be yours by calling 1-800-396-0099 or by visiting their Web site at **www.golfsmith.com**.

Pro Golf

Pro Golf has been around for more than 30 years but has grown with the latest wave of golf enthusiasm and by franchising outlets since 1975. They now sport about 165 locations in the United States (in 35 states) plus locations in Canada and the Philippines. Stores range from 4,000 to 20,000 square feet and offer a full line of golf products. Pro Golf's prices usually are good because they buy in such huge quantities. They also have a semiannual catalog and a new Internet site at **www.progolf-discount.com**. Catalogs can be ordered by calling 1-800-PROGOLF or visiting their Web site at **www.progolf-discount.com**.

The Shopping Experience

When shopping for golf equipment, you should look for knowledgeable sales people who listen to your needs and do not simply try to sell you the hottest items off the rack. The bigger superstores have the widest assortment and usually have a well-trained staff. You might find, however, that the staff at a golf course pro shop has more time to ascertain your particular needs. Some golfers buy many of the basics from larger stores but have specific clubs fit by a golf professional to round out their sets. Others research what they want thoroughly and then take the time to shop around to find the best prices. Combining desired features with a price point at which they are comfortable is how many golfers select their equipment. Some see what they want and simply buy it, but others do research or seek out guidance.

Internet or Catalogs?

Both the Internet and catalogs provide means for golf shopping. Along with some of the major retailers previously listed, a wealth of companies have products you can purchase online. Unless you know specifically what you want from shopping around, however, it can be more difficult to get a feel for a club or the comfort of a shirt when buying over the Internet. Although shopping online saves you the need to leave home, it also means waiting until the product arrives and hoping it arrives in the proper condition. As is always the case online, unless you are shopping on the Web site of a major retailer or even a manufacturer, carefully double-check the source from which you are buying. Also check to see that the material posted is still available and up to date.

Good old-fashioned catalogs often are preferred because you need not wait to find your site. You can simply flip to the page with the clubs, balls, or bags you want. Pro shops or specialty golf retailers are your best bet as opposed to a department store that might have a page of golf equipment somewhere in the back. Many people use the Internet to gather information but still order catalogs from golf retailers because they feel more comfort and trust placing catalog orders. Why do you think that, in this age of electronics, catalog business is still booming?

Specials

Wherever you shop, you should look for advertised specials, particularly in the off season (which varies depending on where you live) when items might be marked down. Another little trick to golf shopping is similar to that of car shopping. You might want to buy the 1999 models late in the year for less money because the 2000 models have just arrived. Often a line of balls are cheaper only because the newer models have come out, adding a new metal core or a dimple pattern that's supposed to make your ball orbit the moon twice. If you think about it, a mere 10 to 12 months ago, the previous line of balls was supposed to be the new ground-breaker of the game. In other words, the previous models might serve you just as well and cost less.

The PGA Golf Show, held semiannually (in September and February), is the industry's coming-out party at which they introduce their new product lines. This means you can look for new products in the spring or the fall, and you can check the prices on previous lines of balls or clubs.

What Do I Wear?

Golfers have taken lots of ribbing about their attire over the years because the sport has produced some loud (sometimes blaring) and occasionally off-beat fashions. Although many courses have basic dress codes (no shorts, no halters, and so on), most are not overly concerned with your fashion choices—as is obvious by some of the outlandish getups you see golfers wear.

Loose-fitting, comfortable clothes help you form a comfort level, as does the right material for the right region of the country or season of the year. Dressing sharp and wearing the latest styles, not unlike a ballplayer putting on his or her uniform, can make you feel good about how you present yourself on the course. If you feel good, it just might rub off on your game. Confidence is a big part of golf and is a reason why people want to look good. This also spills over into equipment choices.

What you wear also might be connected to who makes up your foursome. If you are looking to impress a client, you might aim to look more stylish than if you simply are playing at a local municipal course with a couple of buddies on your day off.

Some golfers use a typical golfing rule of thumb as their dress code, "Dress better than the starter." The starter is the person who sends you out to your assigned tee time. He or she works at the course and is seen by everyone. Therefore, in some regard, he or she sets the code of dress for that course. Remember, however, that this is just a theory.

Acknowledgments

I'd like to thank the many people involved with the manufacturing of golf equipment, shoes, gloves and clothing, who were helpful in writing this book. Also thank you to some key golf retailers. A special thanks to Jackie Beck at Spalding; Lincoln Cox at Edwin Watts; golf club historian Jeff Ellis; the Professional Clubmakers Society; the folks at Golf Shop Operations magazine; and John Mutch, Frank Thomas, and the fine people at the USGA. Finally, thank you Carol for your patience.

Chapter 1

Golf Balls

One of the most basic elements of golf is the golf ball, which has been one of the most studied, probed, prodded, tested, and carefully measured spheres of the past 400 years. Trying to create the perfect golf ball is one of man's most enduring quests that, to date, remains an ongoing challenge.

In the early 1600s, the ball was a two-piece model not un-like today's, except it was made by hand from two pieces of leather and was stuffed with boiled feathers (quite un-like today). Since that time, thousands of varieties of balls have been invented, tested, and marketed. Thousands more have not made the grade. Ball types have included the old *featheries*, others made from a rubbery substance called gutta percha, and finally, those with a rubber core. This ultimately led to mass production and numerous variations on a theme.

The early part of the 20th century saw golf balls "take off" so to speak. Various golf balls were filled with tiny steel balls, a jelly-like substance, water, and chemicals. Balls were even made with an interior of compressed air. Unfortunately, they tended to explode. By the 1960s, more than

300 golf-ball manufacturers were still working on this age-old quest. Today, thousands of balls are on the market, all of which went through rigorous testing before being put on the shelves.

The Science Behind It All

To give you an idea of the testing complexity and of the vast number of balls being manufactured, the United States Golf Association (USGA) has a list of more than 1900 different balls that conform to the set standards for golf balls. Many of these aren't even on the market yet. To test balls in the USGA's research and testing center, an air gun is used to launch balls. The ball's behavior is studied upon impact such as when the club face meets the ball. Other testing stations determine the velocity of the ball, which is fed into a computer that tests the ball's performance under a variety of circumstances. Balls are then placed in an incubator at a constant temperature for three hours before being tested for size and weight. And on it goes, not only at the USGA but at ball manufacturers worldwide. Just for the record

> Golf balls cannot exceed 1.68 inches in diameter, cannot weigh more than 1.62 ounces, cannot fly farther than 280 yards (plus a 6-percent tolerance), and cannot go faster than 255 feet per second according to the USGA.

For the purposes of the typical golfer, the bulk of this golf-ball information rivals that of a science class and is just about as useful. The bottom line for the average golfer is to find a ball that provides distance and durability and has the right feel—at a good price. More advanced golfers also consider weather, course conditions, and even the characteristics of the clubs they are using.

Most golf balls today are of two varieties: the two-piece solid ball or the wound ball. There also are three- and even four-piece balls available. Generally, the average player uses a two-piece solid ball that tends to be rather durable and that allows for greater distance. Two-piece balls are designed with various center cores. Although there are far fewer wound balls on the market, these balls generally offer a softer feel and are more responsive around the green. A wound ball allows for greater control, but it is not as durable as its two-piece solid counterpart. In fact, a wound ball can lose its shape over time, but it's more likely that you'll lose the ball long before that happens.

Covers

In addition to the brand being printed on it, the cover material also is of significance. Most balls have synthetic covers made of surlyn, lithium surlyn, or similarly manufactured materials, while others are covered with a softer material called balata. The leading ball makers, such as Wilson, Spalding, Bridgestone, and others, have been able to make covers (including double covers) that are very tough for distance but soft enough to allow you some spin for the short game. Double covers allow for both distance and finesse by placing a softer cover over a hard one.

The surface of most modern balls should no longer cut, even after extensive use. The dimple patterns, which emerged in 1905 and have been rearranged and reconfigured millions of times since, allow for far greater trajectory than a smooth ball. Under similar launch conditions, according to the USGA, a smooth ball carries 120 yards compared to a dimpled ball, which carries 260 yards. Most golf balls have between 392 and 432 dimples; however, the number of dimples is a less significant factor in the performance or flight of a ball than the pattern and dimensions.

For the average golfer, the number, pattern, and dimensions of the dimples do not matter greatly. Perhaps more significant is the fact that deeper dimples create a lower trajectory with less carry and more roll, while shallower dimples create a higher carry and less roll. Symmetric dimple patterns allow for greater accuracy. With this in mind, companies use very well-tested (often similar) dimple numbers and patterns, all of which are symmetrical.

Core

Almost all solid golf balls are made with a core of synthetic rubber. Companies strive to find the liveliest rubber, the one with the highest initial velocity off the club's face. The core, in conjunction with the cover, dictates the distance. Because golf balls have weight-limit specifications, companies have to be careful when selecting material to fill the core. They want to meet the weight specifications while providing the lightest ball and the most distance. Cores today are filled with materials such as zinc oxide, calcium carbonate, titanium, tungsten, or a liquid. Each company will tell you why their core is the best ever created, and since you are not about to slice open the ball and take it to a science lab to have it thoroughly examined (the USGA does that for you), you basically have to take their word about why they use their material of choice.

Spin

Another factor in the quest for the perfect golf ball is the *spin factor*. High-spin balls can be easier to control on your short game because they give you more backspin and stopping action. The ball has a higher trajectory, less distance, and less roll. On a short par three or en route to a small, fast, or elevated green, a high-spin ball can be advantageous. When smacking away for distance off the tee on a 560-yard par five, however, a low-spin ball travels lower, farther, and has more roll.

Less side spin also is beneficial to people who slice or hook the ball too often. It would be nice if you could switch balls during the hole, but the rules say you cannot. This means you cannot drive with a low-spin ball and then switch to a higher-spin ball when you get closer to the green. You can, however, use a different ball for each hole.

Compression

When reading golf-ball ads or packages—and you should check a few because this is the only way to discern between the multitude of balls on the market—you'll probably notice the term *compression*. This essentially means how hard the ball is inside. Technically speaking, it is a measure of how much force it takes to deflect the ball under a static load. The number, however, is not an actual unit of measurement. Most balls are between 90 and 100, with 90 having a slightly softer feel and 100 feeling like a rock on a cool day. The difference for the average golfer (according to a USGA spokesperson) is almost indeterminate, a few feet in distance. Balls that measure 92 in compression are rounded to 90; those at 97 or 98 can be rounded to 100, making the difference even smaller.

Compression was a greater factor when balls primarily were wound. The compression reflected how tightly the ball was wound. If anything, compression works in conjunction with swing speed. Faster speeds hit high-compression balls more effectively, and lower-compression balls (80) are better for players with a slower swing speed. Nonetheless, many typical golfers see 80, 90, and 100 compression balls and simply reach for the 90s because they are the middle number.

Golf Balls for Everyone

As is the case with everything else as we head into the next millennium, there are numerous golf balls from which to choose. Balls are being manufactured for different types of players and to cater to varying golfer's needs.

To allow for a higher flight from the ball or to get a higher trajectory, for example, a senior might play a lighter ball, which also is made to be more efficient at slower swing speeds. Technology is even creating hybrid balls that combine the properties of the wound ball with the properties of the solid ball, offering control and a softer feel while also allowing for distance.

Temperature

Golf balls should be kept somewhere warm. A ball is constructed to best perform in terms of distance and trajectory when the temperature is between 75 and 90 degrees. Extreme cold affects wound balls somewhat but should not make a great difference on a two-piece surlyn ball, although the ball will feel dramatically harder. It's recommended to keep balls in the warmth of the golf bag, but it is not recommended to actually heat a golf ball because it can lose its properties.

Planning

Golfers often pull an older, cheaper, or *range ball* from their bags when faced with a forced carry over water. Range balls are balls that because of some slight defect are sold more cheaply by manufacturers as company rejects. They generally don't fly as far and can bounce or roll awkwardly. Although this saves you from losing your better ball, it also might be setting you up for disaster because the better ball might have the trajectory to clear the water hazard.

Although you might not have, or even need, the ball expertise to select the right ball for each hole—you want to keep your concentration on other aspects of your game—you might select a different brand or style of ball before approaching a particular course. A long 7,200-yard course with long par fives will differ from a shorter course with elevated greens and a need for finesse. A course with fast greens might require a ball that spins higher and that stops on the green. If you're buying balls at the pro shop prior to heading onto the course, you might inquire about which ones best suit that particular course and then factor in your game.

Making Some Sense of it All

What does this all mean? It means you should look for a ball that meets one or maybe two basic needs of your game—be it distance, better control, or greater spin for your short game. Look at the blurbs, look for the brand names, and look at the prices. Many golfers start by simply buying the popular brand name that's on sale. Golf balls generally vary between $15 and $55 for a dozen, with most name brands landing in the $35 to $45 range. You also can buy a sleeve, which is 3 or 4 balls, or larger packages of 12 to 20 balls offered by most companies. *Control* and *feel* balls often are a little higher priced than the more common *distance* balls. You might want to start with several sleeves of different balls and do your own comparison test to determine which one helps you achieve the best distance, the best control, or the best feel for the money. Various stores and sites online sell used balls that, if they're fairly recent models from well-known companies, can be just as good as the new ones. There is, however, a good feeling that a golfer gets when teeing up a brand new ball.

How Many?

Starting a round of golf with two dozen balls should give you more than you need. Never be too discouraged when you lose one—that's part of the game. Even the pros lose balls on the course.

If you're serious about the game, you should always stock up on golf balls whenever you can. Anytime there's a sale on a ball you particularly like, buy a couple dozen and hang onto them.

Always know what ball you're playing. There are hundreds of brands out there, but it's always good to be sure which ball is yours—especially when you get to the green and three Titleists are sitting two, five, and nine yards from the green.

A Wide Variety of Golf Balls

Golf balls are manufactured worldwide in countries such as Australia, Austria, Belgium, Canada, France, Germany, Japan, Korea, Malaysia, The Netherlands, Republic of China, South Africa, Thailand, and The United Kingdom as well as here in the United States. As of 1998, more than 1,900 balls conform to USGA standards, and the list continues to grow rapidly. Not all 2,000 are on the shelves at present, but there still are many from which to choose.

The first thing you'll notice when shopping for golf balls is the brand name. This is only natural because it's prominently featured on the packaging. Among the most common names are Titleist, Top Flite from Spalding, Precept from Bridgestone, Maxfli from Dunlop, and Wilson. As of 1999, other major equipment makers such as Taylor Made and Cobra are now also in the golf ball game, along with the shoe giant Nike. Callaway also should have balls available soon.

The following sections contain the lowdown on some of the balls you'll find on the shelves. Remember, the best way to judge the best golf ball for your game is to determine what is most important to you: driver distance (low-spin, usually solid balls), 8-iron spin/ability to stop on the green (high-spin balls), feel (softer covers for control), or durability (cover material—most are very similar). Manufacturers now make balls that offer everything under the sun. Check the ratings or take the maker's word for it. Look for properties you need and ignore the hype such as *unequaled distance* or *ultra soft*. Comparatively speaking, a golf ball will never be *ultra soft*.

HPG—Ram Tour

Separated from the Ram Club division in 1993, Ram Tour Golf Balls specializes in making a variety of golf balls for a host of needs. Long-time forerunners in the technology of balls, they were the first to add surlyn to the cover of the ball and have more recently created the only seamless dimple pattern that allows for striking the ball anywhere and having it perform the same way. Of course, this is only discernible to the top-level players. Nonetheless, Ram Tour Golf Balls feature their latest innovative line including the XV2, Balata LB, and Reactive models.

> **Ram Tour XV2.** Direct from the chem lab, this modern three-piece ball incorporates neodymium, titanium, and magnesium. These give the ball an extremely quick start off the club face, greater energy transfer under impact, and a soft feel. The ball is built for durability, distance, and feel. What more do you want?

> **Ram Tour Balata LB.** This two-piece ball also sports metal technology. The combined titanium and balata cover is designed to add feel and control without sacrificing distance.

> **Ram Tour Reactive.** Made in conjunction with the new breed of titanium woods, the Tour Reactive is designed to react, or *explode*, off the club face. The ball should respond to the hard surface of the club face by giving you less spin, more distance, and greater roll.

> **Ram Tour Extrava Lite.** This new two-piece ball is designed to be lighter and more reactive to swing speeds under 80 mph. The ball spins less and should provide straighter, longer shots with more roll. It's a good choice for seniors who might have lost a few miles per hour on their swings.

Maxfli

Maxfli, part of the Dunlop Maxfli Corporation, has been receiving a great deal of attention of late because their *Revolution*, an aptly named new ball, has become the ball of choice for a number of tour professionals. The company boasted 27 tour wins in 1998 with their golf balls. Equally impressive has been their dedication to future stars of the game as they sponsor the PGA Junior Championship.

Although they are returning to the club market this year, Maxfli places a major emphasis on creating technologically advanced golf balls for increased power, better feel, and more or less spin depending on which you desire. Their corporate partner in South Carolina, Dunlop, has been busy in the lab working with magnesium and titanium to advance their own brand name of popular golf balls as well.

> **Maxfli Tour Patriot.** The Tour Patriot is a new long-distance ball with a wound ball feel. Using wound ball technology, the Patriot has a layered construction around a large solid core, and is wrapped in a thin layer of elastic for better control. Geared for mid to high handicappers, the ball will give added distance, but should help maintain a sense of control.
>
> **Maxfli HT.** A circle thread-winding pattern and a brand new Urethane cover provide tour-caliber spin on this new entry from Maxfli. The ball is designed to be durable with a soft feel for control and precision shot making.
>
> **Maxfli Revolution.** A three-piece multipurpose ball with multilevel technology, the Revolution is designed to enhance the game of better players by giving them a little extra in each area. A soft urethane cover and an elastic middle layer provide feel and control. A large solid core also is included to enhance distance.

Maxfli MD Tungsten. Three different compressions (80, 90, and 100) include different amounts of tungsten in the core for different weights. The idea is for golfers with a faster swing speed to use the 100 compression and golfers with a slower swing speed to use the 80 compression to get airborne faster.

Maxfli XS Distance. For mid to high handicappers, this two-piece solid ball is designed to give you the most yardage for your money, or bang for your buck. A 402-dimple aerodynamic design was created to help keep you on the fairway provided you hit it relatively straight.

Dunlop Titanium (Ti) Distance. This ball uses a titanium dioxide additive in the cover blended with surlyn. The heavier cover lowers the moment of inertia, reduces spin, and thus increases distance. A 392-dimple pattern was designed to improve the aerodynamics of the ball. There's also a distance ball for juniors with a lighter, lower compression more suitable for junior swing speeds.

Dunlop Magnesium (MG) Spin. If you're sick of titanium balls, this MG uses a magnesium additive in the cover. When mixed with surlyn, it produces a softer, thinner cover for greater spin and greater control.

Nike

Because everyone else is in the golf ball market, Nike figured why not join the field. Between the Nike tour and their already successful marketing and advertising efforts, it won't be difficult for the Oregon-based sportswear giant to establish themselves as golf ball makers as well. In February 1999, Nike's golf balls were officially introduced with two main goals: to provide players with greater accuracy, and to help consumers learn which ball is right for them. Although diehard Titleist, Top Flite, or Precept players might already know which ball is right for their games, there are still many people out there willing to try something new. As of 1999, the Nike golf ball line consists of four choices.

> **Nike's Precision Tour Control.** This is Nike's *feel* and *finesse* wound ball, designed with a solid core for higher spin and a soft cover for precision putting. This also is the highest priced of the line, costing around $45 per dozen.

> **Nike's Precision Spin Control.** Also in the control and accuracy category, this spin ball has a high-energy core to amplify impact but a soft cover for *feel*.

> **Nike's Precision Distance Control.** Less side spin helps you stay on the fairways; higher iron back swing helps you hug the green. For the most part, this ball leans toward distance, as the name indicates, with greater draw and fade.

> **Nike's Precision Distance.** A durable long-distance ball, this new one is designed with reduced side spin for accuracy. The main purpose, however, is maximum distance and lots of roll to help you shorten those par five, 500 yarders. At around $25 per dozen, this is the least expensive ball in the new Nike line.

Precept

Bridgestone Sports, makers of Precept golf balls, clubs, and accessories, is a subsidiary of Bridgestone Sports, Japan. This company is the largest manufacturer of golf balls in Japan and has been around since the early 1900s. It has only been around in the United States since the late 1980s, but it has quickly established itself among the leaders in golf ball sales, thanks to innovative technology.

In 1993, the Precept EV Extra Spin caught on as a high-performance, two-piece golf ball and gained attention with the success of Nick Price on the PGA Tour.

The latest line of balls from Precept is the MC balls, which feature Muscle-Fiber Core (MC) technology. This technology incorporates new materials that bond the rubber molecules in the core closer together, making a tighter bond that minimizes the loss of energy transferred between the club head and the ball. In short, the new rubber-core technology allows for both greater distance and a softer feel.

Precept MC Double Cover Distance & Spin. The Cadillac of the Precept line, this new performance golf ball combines ultimate distance with an excellent feel and a high spin rate around the green. The inner cover is designed for distance with a softer surlyn cover over it for the right *feel*. The ball was used by the winner of the 1998 US Open, Lee Janzen.

Precept MC Distance. A larger muscle-fiber core allows for greater distance in this two-piece ball that also has a higher spin for a softer feel and more precise control around the green.

Precept MC Spin. The MC Distance also is a two-piece ball with the muscle-fiber core. It is designed with an extra soft, high-spin surlyn cover.

Precept Dynawing. A double-cover ball, this three-piece ball is designed for distance at any club head speed. The two covers, however, also provide a softer feel for better control on approach shots. This ball has seen a good amount of use on the PGA and LPGA pro tours.

Precept MC Lady & MC Senior. Both balls are designed for maximum performance at lower club head speeds. The cover is 13 percent thinner than previous Precept models for added distance, and the high-performance surlyn cover allows for a good feel around the green.

Slazenger

Nearly a century after introducing products in Great Britain for lawn tennis and establishing themselves as an international multisport manufacturer, Slazenger founded their golf division in the late 1980s. Within a decade, they have established themselves as a major player in the golf market, particularly in the area of golf balls. Their two-piece and three-piece wound balls are carefully tested, and the Slazenger 420 line of balls and their new 408dr series can be found at nearly 8,000 pro shops nationwide.

> **Slazenger's 408dr Raw-Distance 3.** Titanium in the cover and in the core combine to produce a harder, more durable cover with less spin and a faster launch speed; while a new aerodynamic, 408-dimple design adds better lift, less drag, and an all around longer straighter shot—hence the name *Raw Distance* for the top-of-the-line new ball from Slazenger.

> **Slazenger's 420p Power-Control.** If you mix titanium and magnesium, look out. The two minerals in the cover core produce a ball with distance, feel, and a mid trajectory. The combination ball, with a large core and a thin cover, should give you a mix of power and control.

> **Slazenger's 420t Tour-Calibre.** A softer, lighter cover (thanks to magnesium) is designed to provide more backspin and greater control. This is one of the *feel* balls in the 420 series.

> **Slazenger's 420s Select.** Another *feel* ball from Slazenger, the Select is for *select* players … the better ones. A three-piece wound ball with a liquid center, this one is built for feel, spin, and greater distance than the typical wound ball.

> **Slazenger's 420 Interlok.** For the golf purest who values precision and careful shot making, this is

your classic three-piece balata ball. It does, however, come with a modern dimple pattern of interlocking triangles for the desired trajectory. This new line is geared more toward better players.

Titleist

A subsidiary of the Acushnet Company, Titleist has been the leading ball choice at the US Open for the past 50 years and has been a staple on the PGA and LPGA tours, boasting numerous tournament wins annually. In the 1930s, Titleist was the first to freeze liquid centers and x-ray golf balls. Today, they've moved full-throttle forward in technical innovations with their Titleist Launch Monitor, a sophisticated portable computer and camera system designed to measure speed, launch angle, and spin rate. The result of their efforts has made a major market impact. At golf course pro shops, they boast a 50-percent market share, selling half the balls bought anywhere in the United States.

Often considered the standard by which other balls are judged, Titleist makes balls for every style of play from advanced wound balls for accuracy to three-piece, low-spin distance balls, high-spin balls, and extra-distance balls. Titleist also provides performance indicators for driver distance, 8-iron spin, feel, and cover durability whenever you buy a dozen or a sleeve. Essentially, this tells you which ball you should use for each shot. Of course, as previously noted, you can't change the ball for every shot. You have to choose a ball based on the hole and based on which parts of your game you have the most and least confidence.

> **Titleist Professional.** Popular on the pro tours, this is a durable wound ball featuring a liquid-filled center and an enhanced winding process designed to produce lower spin and greater distance. Offering a little bit of everything, the new *Elastomer* synthetic cover also is designed to allow a soft feel around the green.

Titleist Tour Balata. This balata-covered, high-spin, three-piece ball, which is complete with a liquid-filled core, has all the makings of a ball made for precise shot making and expert control. This is a control/feel ball.

Titleist Tour Prestige. Another in the line of "soft" golf balls designed for "feel" and control, the new Tour Prestige is a thicker-walled, thermoplastic liquid-centered ball built for enhanced shot making ability. The ball has an Elastomer cover, making it more durable and longer lasting if you don't lose it. The Tour Prestige has already become a staple in the bags of a number of PGA pros.

Titleist Tour Distance. This ball is designed for exceptional distance. The surlyn cover makes the ball durable, but because it's a wound ball, it maintains a soft feel.

Titleist HP2 Tour and HP2 Distance. The HP2 Tour is a two-piece ball designed to offer a balance of distance and soft-wound-ball feel with good shot-stopping capability. The HP2 Distance is built for durability and longer, straighter shots with a significantly lower driver spin rate off the tee.

Titleist DT Wound and DT 2-Piece. Several hundred million of the DT series have been sold worldwide. The wound ball has a softer feel; the two-piece offers greater distance and is designed to help minimize hooks and slices. Both balls have lithium surlyn covers for durability.

The Acushnet Company, owned by Fortune Brands, also is the maker of the Pinnacle line of balls that has made use of the recent titanium wave with their new Pinnacle Titanium Extreme. The Extreme has a titanium core and a cut-proof cover designed to take off with increased velocity and to travel farther than the competition, thanks to a low spin rate. The Pinnacle Gold LS, Pinnacle Equalizer, and Equalizer For Women also are solid low-spin, lighter-weight balls designed to provide greater length without overswinging. Pinnacles can be had in packs of 15 at good prices.

Top Flite

Top Flite is part of Spalding Sporting Goods Worldwide, which has been in the golf business for a long time. Because Spalding introduced Top Flite, they have been among the leaders in the golf ball industry. Led by the recent Strata series, Top Flite balls are played by more than 200 golf professionals on the four major tours (PGA, LPGA, Senior, and Nike) and by millions of typical golfers worldwide. The Strata series boasted nearly 20 tour victories in 1998. A tungsten core and titanium covers are the latest technological advances used in an attempt to better conform to USGA weight regulations while still giving the player the best ball for distance. The idea is that a small amount of tungsten (a heavier material) can bring the weight limit up while still allowing most of the core to consist of synthetic rubber. The rubber makes it livelier so it will travel farther off the club face.

> **Top Flite Strata Tour.** The multilayer Strata Tour, the latest in the line, is designed for top amateurs and professionals, but this doesn't mean you can't give it a try. It also doesn't mean you'll suddenly start playing like Lee Trevino or Payne Stewart. The ball combines a high-energy core with a soft balata outer cover. It has a spin rating that ranges from high to low, providing distance but also helping with your short game.

> **Top Flite Aero.** This is an aerodynamically unique ball featuring 332 noncircular, teardrop, and ellipsoid-shaped dimples on the cover with a soft feel. The ball is carefully designed to defy wind and air resistance and to travel farther off your driver or irons.

Top Flite Bi-Metal. The Bi-Metal has titanium on the outside and tungsten on the inside. Like an aluminum baseball bat, it's designed for major distance (and it's legal) so put travel stickers on the side of this new entry in the Top Flite line. The new *Metal Matrix Distance Technology* is Top Flite's way of combining premium distance with a soft feel.

Wilson

Wilson, along with Spalding, has been a household name associated with sporting goods for generations. The focus for the bulk of their equipment, including golf balls, is on helping the average player improve his or her game. There are several lines of Wilson balls including the Ultra 500 and the latest offering, the Staff Titanium series. This series features four balls designed for varying types of players with various handicaps. Wilson was the first to take titanium and work it into the core of the ball. The idea is to bond all the materials in the core of the ball into a cohesive unit, allowing the energy from the club head to be transferred into the same direction at impact. In short, the ball should take off.

Although Wilson does not go after tour players, they do pride themselves on making first-rate golf balls geared to helping the rest of us. Nonetheless, they do have more than 2,000 club professionals across the country playing their latest line of Staff Titanium golf balls.

Wilson offers a wide variety of packaging from 3-ball sleeves to 18- or 20-ball packages. They are found everywhere because they market an enormous number of balls annually. You also can get specialized logo balls to make an added impression or to give as a gift.

Staff Titanium Straight Distance. This ball simply does not spin much off the driver and just keeps on going. It's durable and also has less side spin to help you control slices and hooks. This ball is designed for the 15+ handicap player. Needless to say, it's the best seller.

Staff Titanium Spin. Billed by Wilson as *The Longest Spin Ball*, this ball is designed to provide a softer feel around the green (more spin) without sacrificing distance. In short, the *Spin* ball gives you a little of everything. This is for the 10 to 20 handicap player.

Staff Titanium Double Ti. With plenty of titanium in both the core and the inner of the two covers, this is among the latest offerings from Wilson. The outer cover is soft magnesium surlyn for greater feel. Designed to combine spin, feel, and durability, the ball sports 500 (count 'em) dimples and provides distance and greater control. This is for the 5 to 15 handicap player.

Staff Titanium Balata. One of the only double-cover balata balls, this titanium-core model is designed for greater control, finesse, and feel around the green. This is for the golfer seeking precision or the 0 to 10 handicapper.

Others

Cobra, known for their clubs, now join the ball market with their new Cobra Dista balls. The balls are made with a multi-layer cover around a lightweight core. They are designed to enhance feel and add distance at a variety of swing speeds. There are four models, including the ladies model LDY-75.

Taylor Made also recently introduced their new Inergel Balls, featuring a new material inside that is both soft and super resilient all at once. The ball is designed to have enhanced backspin and fly straighter on a softer trajectory than even a balata ball. Called "Inergel" and featuring "Moisture Block," the line may sound like hair products or sun block, but they are the new technologically-sound golf balls which will give Taylor Made a piece of the competitive ball market. The Inergel Tour is designed for feel and precision; the Inergel Pro for a high spin rate and a little extra distance; and the Inergel Pro Distance is for the player seeking much greater distance.

There are many other balls out there, even some that glow in the dark for night play. It's recommended that, if you are not going with one of the preceding name brands, you try to use a ball that conforms to USGA standards. If you're not playing competitively, it really doesn't matter. But it's simply more fun and more challenging to most people to play a game by the rules and within the guidelines.

Chapter 2

Golf Clubs

In Belgium in the early 1300s, a game called Chole was created that involved a ball being hit on the ground by some sort of stick. The game evolved into golf. The stick evolved into a club, made by hand from two pieces of wood, one attached at a right angle to the bottom of the other, and resembled a modern hockey stick more than a modern golf club.

Clubs had names such as "niblick" and "mashie." By the late 1800s, the first metal woods were actually introduced. They didn't catch on, however, and wooden woods returned until around 1980. The early woods were molded from pieces of wood layered together and shellacked.

Over time, iron was added and *irons* emerged. Irons, or blade clubs, were forged in mills and were pounded into shape. Some even had cavities in the back, although the cavity-backed club did not catch on for many years to come. In fact, according to Jeff Ellis, a golf club historian and author of the book *The Clubmakers Art* (Zephyer Productions), many of the so-called *new* innovations in golf clubs really aren't that new at all. They are the result of advanced technological know-how and better marketing to reintroduce inventions of the late 1800s and early 1900s.

Clubs of Today

The modern golf club is the end result of numerous technological tests. Clubs today are the sum of their components.

Club Heads

Club heads can be standard or oversized, and either *cavity-backed* or *forged*. Oversized clubs have a larger club head and club face which makes it easier to strike the ball, and allows for better results off of poor swings or even mis-hits.

Cavity-back club heads have a cavity dug out of the back of the club head and are specially weighted for accuracy and control. They are made of stainless steel, titanium, and other exotic metals and are designed to give you maximum distance and the desired trajectory. Cavity-back clubs are common because they can be *perimeter weighted* to be more forgiving. This essentially means the club is weighted around the club face in such a manner that allows you to get away with not hitting the ball just right on the *sweet spot*.

Forged club heads, or blades, are solid, old-fashioned club heads that are still around but more often used by the better players. The process of forging a club means that a piece of steel (or whatever material) is pounded into shape. Other clubs can be cast iron, which means there's a mold set, hot liquid metal is poured into it, and it dries into the shape of the club. Forged clubs are stronger, but cast clubs have a softer feel.

Oversized clubs give you more room on the club face to hit the ball, and the perimeter-weighted clubs make more of the club face consistent to give you a decent outcome on a ball that isn't hit in the center of the club. Basically, the sum total of larger club faces and perimeter weighting is to help the majority of golfers who often do not hit the ball on the sweet spot.

Shafts

The shaft is the engine of the club. Shafts usually are made from graphite or steel. The primary difference is—not unlike the ball you're striking—control versus distance. Steel shafts give you greater control and more precision; graphite adds more distance because it's a lighter material that enables you to generate greater club-head speed. Graphite can allow for better shock absorption when the club head meets ball and can be kinder on miss-hits.

Different flexes in shafts range from ones that are more flexible (bend more) to ones that are stiffer. You'll be able to choose the one that best suits your swing. A player with a slower swing speed will want a little more flexibility in the shaft, while a player with a fast swing speed can use a stiffer club. It all goes back to physics—trust me. You need not know the details, simply know which best suits your game.

Grips

Grips are the steering wheel or control portion of the club, and they need to feel comfortable and durable. Most grips today are made from rubber, leather, or one of a couple synthetic materials. There also are cord grips, which are less common but are good all-weather grips. These are slowly becoming more popular with the average player.

Leather grips can feel marvelous, but they are more costly and are not always the best choice in wet or even damp weather. Rubber, which is very popular, can provide the *sticky* grip you need at a more reasonable price. Rubber wears down, however, and should be replaced periodically.

Some synthetic materials also are very popular because they give you a good solid feel for the club and generally are more durable. Synthetic grips can be had for $5 to $10 per club. Grips don't last forever. When you're losing that desired feel or are starting to wear through, it's time to replace them. Pro shops and golf stores can replace grips easily.

Club Sets

When buying a set of clubs, it's important that you have the opportunity to test drive, or at least swing, each club enough times to feel comfortable. Because you can have, according to the rules, up to 14 clubs in your bag, you'll have some choices to make.

Manufacturers make a wide array of drivers (or woods), fairway woods, irons, wedges, and putters for all occasions. Generally, the 1- and 3-wood, a fairway wood or two (perhaps a 4- and/or 5- or 7-), your 2-, 3-, 4-, 5-, 6-, 7-, 8-, and 9-irons, a wedge, a sand wedge, and a putter make up a solid 14-club set.

Some players eliminate a 2- or 3-iron and add another wood to their repertoire. Many players, as they become more proficient at the game, notice that they're not using a particular club and find another to put in it's place. Often, a 2- or 3-iron is hard to master. Therefore, you might replace a hated club with a fairway wood that has a greater loft. If you already have a 4- or 5-wood, you might add another wedge to fill in a gap and to help your short game. Use whatever works best for you.

Ultimately, you want a club you can feel comfortable using from every distance, a variety of lies, and different types of terrain. The worst feeling is to be 187 yards away from the hole, lining up your second shot, and not have a club you feel comfortable hitting with from that distance.

Selecting Clubs

To select clubs, it's important that you work with a pro or a knowledgeable salesperson who has the time to custom fit you to some degree. After all, if you are going to take up a challenging activity, why not start out on the right foot. It's very important for you to choose clubs that are long or short enough for your height and reach. You want to be able to make maximum contact without having to reach, lean, or stretch. It also is very important for you to decide on the best grip for your size hands. You should measure your swing speed with your driver. This will help you determine the loft of the club face on the woods and irons as well as the flexibility of the shaft.

The bottom line is that, if you are buying clubs for the first time or even replacing clubs you've had for years, it's advantageous to get some help finding a good set so that you'll feel comfortable on the course.

Men's and Women's Clubs

Women's and men's clubs are similar in most respects. You'll be choosing the same number of clubs for your bag as well as making the same decisions about which clubs you choose to carry. The primary difference between men's and women's clubs is that men's clubs usually are about one inch longer and therefore slightly heavier. The shafts on women's clubs tend to be a little more flexible to adjust to the swing speed, and the grips are a fraction of an inch smaller in diameter. Women, like men, need to select the clubs best suited to their height and swing speed. Some women prefer a thicker grip, and some men prefer a shorter club. People of all shapes, sizes, and physical makeup play golf. As we approach the new millennium, clubs can certainly be found to accommodate anyone.

A Few Things To Remember

In golf, you will find a great deal of hype and promotion by manufacturers who are competing for your business. Therefore, you need to maintain your perspective as a customer. Below are two things to keep in mind when browsing through the myriad of golf equipment you will find in catalogs, online or in golf shops.

Distance

Golfers, led by manufacturers claims and marketing hype, tend to seek out balls and clubs that enhance distance. Beyond your initial drive, however, on the majority of your shots, you are not simply seeking distance. Particularly on your drive, distance is meaningless if you've hit the ball 250 yards but way out of bounds.

Unlike the driving range, where you can smack them a mile to the right or left, you have to play your next shot or lose a stroke. Only the first two of five shots on a par four or five require distance, and none on a par three should have you muscling the ball. Therefore, on a course with six par threes, only a dozen drives and perhaps eight of your second shots require distance. That comes to only 20 of what might be 80 or 100 (or more) shots for a typical golfer in a round.

Loft and precision can be more important than distance. In fact, a golfer who successfully takes the shorter and steadier route, while not being awe-inspiring to the gallery, often makes the money—particularly in an amateur, corporate, or local tournament in which there's a tendency to try to hit home runs to impress.

Don't Listen to Everyone

Everyone you know and every manufacturer boasts the best clubs (and other equipment) for you. Marketing often is the biggest differential between golf clubs or balls because many overlap in their technology. Each company stamps some new technological name on their latest advances. Some advances over the past 10 years have truly changed the face of the game; others haven't. It's worth your while to read up on new clubs, particularly reviews that tell you whether any of these state-of-the-art advances are really improving anyone's game.

There's a lot happening on the equipment front from golf manufacturers, many of whom saw a drop in sales in 1998 despite increased enthusiasm for the game. Therefore, many are busy hyping what they've come up with. Don't get suckered in. Look for valid claims and features that will benefit your game.

Pricing

A set of clubs can run anywhere from $500 to upwards of $2,000. Many golfers buy a set of clubs and then add a fairway wood, an extra wedge, or perhaps a putter to their set afterwards. Drivers generally can be had for anywhere from $100 to $600, fairway woods run in the $175 to $300 range, and a set of eight irons can range from $500 to $1,500. Wedges run between $70 and $150 each, and a putter can cost between $50 and $200. The prestige of the company, new innovations, and the materials used in the club head, shaft, and the rest of the club dictate the price. New players might pick up a starter set of clubs for $149 and juniors can get their first sets (usually with just 5 clubs) for as low as $49. All of the prices mentioned are rough averages from the major equipment manufacturers. Discount stores, special deals, used equipment and other specials can save you money while hand made specialized clubs can cost you more.

Drivers

Two types of woods dominated most of the 20th century: a laminated maple, which stayed dry in wet weather, and persimmon wood, which, although more temperamental and prone to crack, break, or swell, was the popular choice of club makers.

Today, however, metal is all the rage. Oversized heads made of titanium bi or tri metal technology, *Big Berthas*, *King Cobras*, and a host of graphite shafts make up a wide assortment of drivers from which you can choose.

What you want is a driver that's the right length and weight for you and that provides distance without sacrificing control. You also need to consider the feel and the trajectory. You want a ball that doesn't fly too high or too low, an important factor in selecting the proper loft angle. Club-head lofts generally are found in numbers between 7 and 14 degrees. If your club-head speed is 95 mph, you'll want a loft of around 10. At 90 mph, you want a loft of around 11, increasing a degree with each 5 mph.

A lighter club can make the ball fly farther because you can swing at a faster club-head speed. Golfers today, thanks to graphite shafts, are increasing swing speed without the benefit of eating their Wheaties. Graphite shafts are common today because they are lighter, and the club makers can put an oversized, heavier club head at the end without making the overall weight too high. Be careful, however, not to purchase a club that's too light. Just like a baseball player who selects a bat that's too light, you can throw off your swing and can lose a degree of control. A club that's too light can make it very difficult to maintain a nice, even tempo in your swing because you don't have a good *feel* for what you are swinging. Touring pros sometimes use heavier shafts because they are less concerned with adding distance than maintaining feel and better control.

Length, meanwhile, is a matter of height and, as previously mentioned, the length of your reach. Drivers in the 1970s were 43 inches; today they're 45 inches. This means that, if you've been playing a while and have made the switch over the years, you'll have to stand farther back to compensate and use a flatter, less sweeping swing. You want to be able to feel comfortable and in control of the club. If you've ever watched a child try to swing a golf club that's obviously too long for him, you'll get the idea. He doesn't control the club; it controls him.

Metal woods, the definitive oxymoron of the golf industry, are the name of the game. Wooden woods have gone the way of wooden tennis rackets. Titanium, aluminum, and stainless-steel heads are the leaders in the market. Stainless steel offers more power but is slightly heavier, while aluminum and titanium allow for larger, oversized club faces, which provide a larger sweet spot. The sweet spot is the point on the club face where you want to hit the ball.

Callaway's Big Bertha Driver, which came around in the early 1990s, was a significant development. It's been proven that you can get more distance from the club, not simply from the deep face but from the spring effect. It's one of many well-marketed clubs that have lived up to their praises. Many other clubs are following in Bertha's footsteps with variations on the oversized theme. Some will be beneficial to your game; others are simply well marketed.

Keep in mind that, if you do opt for the popular oversized club heads, you need to adjust to them by teeing the ball up higher. This allows the sweet spot of the larger club face to hit the ball squarely. Teeing it up higher also allows the ball to be hit below the midsection, and you want to hit the ball below its equator for greater lift.

Fairway Woods

For years, golfers toiled away trying to work their mysterious fairway woods. When buying clubs, everyone told you to have a 3- and perhaps a 4-wood in your bag, but you never figured out why. Thanks to modern technology, those hated clubs—often the cleanest in your bag—are now becoming a major part of the game.

Fairway woods, from a 2- to a 9-wood, are now primarily of the metal wood variety with a varying degree of loft. A 4-wood, for example, has about 19 degrees of loft (similar to a 2-iron), a 6-wood has 25 degrees and is closer to an iron, and so on. Swing speed determines how much loft you need.

One reason golfers are now leaning toward the fairway woods over the irons is that the woods have a bigger sweet spot and are being made with a lower center of gravity. This means they strike the bottom part of the ball better, thus lifting it, and your goal is to get the ball airborne. Also, metal woods generally are slightly longer than irons; therefore, you can generate more club-head speed.

Another advantage to buying a fairway wood, particularly if you play courses with lots of rough, is that you'll have more impact when hitting a second (long) shot from the rough.

Simply put, fairway woods can provide more power and more forgiveness.

There are numerous fairway woods from which you can choose. Not unlike the Big Bertha drivers that made a big splash in the market with their oversized club heads a few years back, Adams Golf has more recently come up with a unique club-head design for their Adams Tight Lies series, which strikes the lower half of the golf ball better. Instead of a club face that's bigger on top than on the bottom, Adam's new design has a club face that's larger on the bottom. Needless to say, it's a big hit and has helped make the fairway wood a club of choice. Golfers also are finding that they use some of the fairway woods off the tee as a driver, looking to enhance swing speed and use the higher loft angle.

As for oversized club heads on fairway woods, while they can be advantageous for your drivers, they are not necessarily any better for fairway woods where the ball isn't sitting up nicely on a tee. Midsized and standard sized club heads often work best and are more comfortable for many players who find them easier to control when hitting off the grass. Fairway woods are made from stainless steel, titanium, and other popular club-making materials.

Irons

Irons are the clubs that occupy much of your day and often cause the most frustration. No matter which irons you buy and what the manufacturer claims, it's more important to take time to practice. Many golfers spend time with their woods at the range and with their putters on the putting green but neglect their irons and wedges when it comes to practicing.

Your irons will feature increasing lofts to help you get more trajectory and less roll as you get closer to the green. The lower-number irons (1- through 3-) traditionally have been the toughest clubs to hit. This explains why many golfers are now seeking solace in the new-and-improved fairway woods.

Many irons today are being designed with the typical golfer in mind. These irons are made with a carved-out-cavity back and an oversized head. The idea is to try to make it easier for the average player to hit with irons. Unlike the oversized club heads on the drivers, however, oversized irons aren't always as favorable because, like the fairway woods, you are hitting off the grass, particularly the rough. In simple terms, although you have more club face with which to strike the ball, you also have more club face with which to strike the grass and rough. Irons have to work out of all sorts of lies on the course including hills, tall grass, damp terrain, and so on.

You want a sense of control, which for some people means a medium-size club face. While a larger club face will be more forgiving, which is appreciated by newer players, more advanced players feel they can better work the smaller club head to meet the ball more precisely.

To help you, the sole (or bottom) of many irons is now carefully designed to work comfortably from any type of lie or terrain. The heel to toe is no longer flat but shaped to decrease ground friction at impact. More often, clubs feature rounded edges to help against wind resistance and create less resistance when striking the grass. Rounded clubs are actually not new, with many clubs in the 1920's having a similar look. A bounce angle also is factored in, which determines how well the club will respond to hitting the ground. You don't want a club digging into the ground. The better golfers can match up the sole and bounce angle of a club to the manner in which they swing.

Perimeter weighting means the cavity in the back of the club head is weighted around the outer part of the head rather than behind the center back portion. The balanced weight around the outer portion of the club head can help prevent twisting and turning at impact and can help you when you do not hit the ball in the center of the club face. On the other hand, because the club is designed to work well for the golfer who does not always hit the ball squarely, it might not be as proficient for the more skilled golfer who *does* hit iron shots with the middle of the club face more consistently. Therefore, some better players will opt for the more traditional irons.

Such "traditional" irons, or blades, are still around. These are straight-back irons with no special weight distribution. They are the clubs that were around for years until the new irons showed up. The choice of irons is yours, depending on how well you can handle them and depending on what works best for you in terms of getting the ball in the air (and hitting it straight) consistently.

Irons generally are not *power clubs* because you are not always looking to muscle the ball. Finesse and control are a significant part of your iron game. If you need to hit a shot 130 yards to reach the green, you need to use the iron that will hit it that far for you. If your 7-iron is billed as a club that will hit 150 yards, it's not going to help you. Essentially, if it lives up to it's billing, you'll be over the green. Therefore, you need to think, "What will get me to the green?" when selecting your irons.

Roughly speaking, for irons, the distances will vary depending on the player and the club. Nonetheless, here's a rough chart:

> 2-iron, from 170 to 200 yards
>
> 3-iron, from 150 to 180 yards
>
> 4-iron, from 140 to 170 yards
>
> 5-iron, from 130 to 160 yards

6-iron, from 120 to 150 yards

7-iron, from 100 to 140 yards

8-iron, from 90 to 130 yards

9-iron, from 70 to 110 yards

As you can see, there is an overlap. How well you hit with a certain club, wind, and the lie of the ball will be the determining factors when deciding which club to use.

Wedges

One or two of the most important and least talked about clubs in your bag are your wedges. They are your partners on the course from 125 yards to the green. They can put you in one, two, three, or more putting range. A player who is proficient with a wedge can place his third shot onto the green within a few feet of the pin for a par four. A loft or gap wedge to place you from the fairway close to the pin is important, as is a sand wedge to get you out of those traps!

Choosing the right wedges is a matter of selecting the amount of loft and bounce you want. Loft angles have changed over the years. Most pitching wedges are in the 47 to 52 degree range, sand wedges are in the mid 50s, and lob wedges check in around 60 degrees. It's important to have irons and wedges covering as much of a range of lofts as possible so that, as you approach the green, you'll be better able to land the ball on the green squarely and without much roll. Another way to look at it is to ask yourself, "Do I have a club that I feel comfortable hitting the ball with from every distance range?" Club makers, taking this into account, continue to create more wedges to fill in the gaps they create by changing the loft angles. Don't fall for this sales technique and feel compelled to buy a series of new-fangled wedges for every 10 yards from 120 to the green. A good golfer does not try to solve every course challenge with his or her equipment; he learns to utilize the clubs in the bag. Remember, you can only carry 14 clubs, so don't go out and buy five wedges for every 15 yards from 75 to the green. Learn to use your wedge properly.

Basically, you want a wedge that will feel comfortable when swinging in a bunker and one that will feel comfortable on the fairway. Similar to the irons, the bounce on the sole of the club is how much the club will react against the ground. Bounce ranges from around 2 to 13 with 2 being the smallest amount. Players generally seek out more bounce (like a 12) when hitting out of the sand so club will hit through the sand and not dig in. On the other end is a shot from the fairway with little bounce (like a 2). Sand wedges also are slightly heavier to combat the resistance of the sand. Go for a higher bounce angle for your sand wedge and less for your pitching wedge.

Wedges often are about 10 inches shorter than drivers. Your club length should decrease consistently from your driver down to your wedges. You must be able to swing comfortably. Control with a wedge is vital. Many players look for a wedge with which they can pinch the ball, almost like pinching a marble between your finger and a carpet thus making it pop up. With a wedge, the loft angle should pinch, or pop, in the right direction with backspin to keep it from rolling away.

Putters

Calamity Jane, Blue Goose, Type Mallet, Schenectady, Bobby Grace, Cash-In, and other names have been used for putters over the years. A few nicknames we can't print also have been heard around the course when this little club has turned a par into a double bogey.

Long drives and splendid iron and approach shots with your wedge all can go for naught if you cannot putt. Although a good putter won't teach you how to line up a putt or read the green, it does help to have a club in which you have confidence and on which you can rely when trying to sink your putts.

Don't forget that golf is 90 percent mental, particularly when putting.

There are three types of putters: mallet, blade, or toe heel weighted. Before the newer weighted putters hit the golf market, there were mallet putters dating back to the early 1900s. These are the putters with a rounded back and a large club head. Blade putters have two faces off a straight blade and a bull's-eye. The most popular putters today are the toe-heel weighted variety because they tend to keep the putter head on line. They also are more forgiving if you don't hit the ball exactly where you want.

Toe-heel weighting is designed for various putting styles, but mallets and blades are more a matter of comfort and choice (with mallets being slightly heavier). All are prominently found on any golf course.

Today, you can find numerous variations on these basic putting themes. There are oversized heads, longer and shorter shafts, and varying-performance club faces, which include graphite, aluminum, ceramic, nickel, steel, tungsten, bronze, brass, and other materials.

The last few years have seen various insert materials in putters in an attempt to make the ball feel softer coming off the face. The most important aspect of the putter, after all, is *feel*. A softer carbon milling in the face of the club is one of many materials designed to make the ball feel just right off the club face. John Mutch of the USGA says that nearly half of all clubs the USGA makes rulings on are putters, determining whether they fit within the specifications as set forth by the rules. There are all sorts of models from which you can choose.

One of the most significant factors for determining which type of putter you should choose is your style of putting. Putting styles vary more than any other part of the game. Why? Because it's a simple stroke that doesn't require any great strength or a special type of swing. It's a stroke anyone can do at his or her favorite miniature golf course, on the rug at your office, or on your back patio.

Reading the green is done in preparation for the putt, but it does not involve the actual club. The basic principle of meeting the ball and hitting it, a little harder or softer, is still the same. Once you've established how you putt, you can pick out a club that best suits you. Keep in mind your height in relation to your putting style and buy a putter that fits accordingly. Putters generally range from 32 to 36 inches. There are longer putters, exceeding 40 inches as well. While only 5 percent of golfers use them, they are beneficial to golfers who have not had good luck with other types of putters, or players who have back problems and would prefer not to have to bend to putt.

Yes, you can get some loft on your putter should you play on greens that are slow, or worn, or that need extra oomph behind your putt. Most golfers, however, do not think too much about loft on their putter.

Ultimately, the putter that feels best in your hands and that meets the ball squarely is the one for you. It's a matter of comfort and feel.

So Many Clubs To Choose From

The following sections discuss some of the numerous clubs on the market today from some of the leading club manufacturers. You'll see them in your favorite pro shop or at your nearby golf retailer. Buying a set of one brand can be less expensive and can save you the trouble of mixing and matching.

In many cases, *starter* sets are offered. These might give you anything from 2-woods, 3-irons, and a putter to 11 clubs and a golf bag for under $400. If you are just starting out, this is one way for you to determine whether you like the game.

On the other hand, you might note that different manufacturers specialize in different clubs. Callaway and Cobra, for example, are known for their drivers, Adams for their fairway woods, Cleveland and Mizuno for their irons and Odyssey, Ping, and Teardrop for their putters. You might want to buy a set of irons (often including wedges), as many golfers do, but then select the woods and/or putter from a different company.

Most of the following clubs come with a choice of graphite or steel shafts, a choice of loft faces (even where not indicated), and a choice of flexes. Men's and women's models usually are offered by most companies as are right-handed and left-handed models.

Adams

If you do something very well, why not make it your primary focus of attention. That's the story behind Adams. A growing company, Adams has become the definitive word in fairway woods with their patented design; so much so that they were ranked fifth in *Inc. Magazine*'s 1998 list of the 500 fastest-growing companies. Their Tight Lies fairway woods sold over a million clubs in less than two years.

The club is designed in a revolutionary manner, placing the center of gravity below the equator of the ball so that, when you strike it, you'll get the ball up. Traditionally, club heads are larger on top and smaller on the bottom. Adams has essentially turned the club head upside down to give you maximum hitting area where it counts. It's a significant technological breakthrough in that the club head is not heavier by being weighted at the lower portion. It is simply inverted.

The Tight Lies line includes the 2-, 3-, 5-, 7-, 9-, and 11-irons with different lofts to coincide with different club-head speeds. Because of the loft face and easy handling, some people use the 2-iron as a driver to give them added lift. Club heads are steel, and shafts are either steel or graphite with a variety of flexes from which to choose. The clubs are relatively light but not so much so that you lose efficiency.

Adams makes other clubs, most notably their new SC Series Titanium Drivers, and their new Nick Faldo Series Wedges. The SC Series Titanium Drivers include an oversized forged titanium head and lightweight graphite shaft. Adams has designed the clubs with the idea of controlling spin for longer and straighter tee shots. The clubs are made with what Adams describes as a "complex bulge design which incorporates a controlled relationship between the club face and the center of gravity to optimize spin." The optimized spin should increase distance. The SC drivers come in three models designed for different types of players, including those who carefully work the ball; those who slice; and, of course, those who hook.

The Nick Faldo Wedges honor the world famous golfer with a series of three wedges—pitch, sand, and open face finesse models. All three of the stylishly crafted clubs are built to have a softer feel and are available in 56- and 60-degree lofts with gold steel shafts and Lamkin Crossline grips. With some direction from Nick himself, the clubs should make life easier for you from a variety of difficult lies.

Bridgestone

From the folks at Bridgestone, who make the popular Precept golf balls, comes a new, oversized, 275 cubic centimeter, forged-titanium club head on their latest driver, the Tera (250cc is more common). Weight distribution for distance and a design that enhances control also are features of the new Tera. Precept also offers the EX Men's Woods with 1-, 3-, and 5-drivers along with the EX Lady's line (which also includes a 7-wood). The EX Senior Woods are popular with senior golfers because they are designed to help increase club-head speeds.

The Precept line of titanium irons, or EX Ti Irons, are oversized and perimeter weighted to be more forgiving.

The graphite shafts are available in different degrees of flex (or stiffness), and the series runs from the 2- through 9-irons plus both a pitching wedge and a sand wedge. Also from Precept are the men's and ladies' Ex Irons, which feature stainless-steel heads and *power rib designs*. In layman's terms, this means that the club should provide a solid feel upon impact, should not twist when you hit the ball, and should give you distance. The sleek-looking series is available in various shafts for varying club-head speeds. The ladies' series starts at the 4-iron and also includes the two wedges.

Callaway

Few pieces of athletic equipment can match the incredible success of the Big Bertha series of oversized woods that first hit the golf world in 1991. Nonetheless, Callaway has taken a bold step forward, making some club face changes and introducing the new Great Big Bertha Hawk Eye series, combining titanium and tungsten in a super light club face with an oversized design allowing more forgiveness. The clubs are also designed to help get the ball airborne easier and with a dramatically low center of gravity. The Hawk Eye line extends from a driver through a series of fairway woods, which are all intended to give you the proper trajectory for your shot. The Hawk Eyes are also built with a light—yet very strong—graphite shaft, plus an increased diameter tip to provide additional strength.

Callaway's Big Bertha Steelhead Fairway Woods sport a large club head, a deeper face, and a lower center of gravity thanks to a new internal weighting system. The club provides more room above the center of gravity so that the ball performs better. An added amount of *bounce* will assist you when the club head meets turf. The line of fairway woods includes the 2- through 9- (called the *divine nine*) and the 11-, all available for both men and women.

Because you need to follow up on your wood shots no matter how far they travel, Callaway has since 1994 featured the Big Bertha line of irons. The Big Bertha X-12 Irons are a stainless-steel series of clubs featuring a low center of gravity to get the ball airborne more easily with the desired trajectory and spin from various distances and lies. The unique multilayer design adds forgiveness for off-center hits. The layers also affect the feel and strength of the club face. A lightweight graphite shaft allows more weight to be in the club head. The idea is to make a club that, even if you don't always strike the ball precisely—which is true for most average golfers—you can still get a good shot. The technology used in the X-12 line picks up where the extremely popular Big Bertha Tungsten-Titanium line of irons left off. They provide both feel and, as Callaway puts it, "exceptional performance under all conditions." The tungsten insert helps decrease twist or any drag on the turf resulting from a solid titanium club head.

The Big Bertha Tour Series Wedges are a four-wedge set featuring the pitching wedge at 48 degrees of loft, the approach wedge at 52, the sand wedge at 56, and the lob wedge at 60 degrees. The club heads are designed in a teardrop shape, making it easier to hit the ball from any position. The wedges also are designed to make shots from tight or difficult lies easier to hit. The Tour Wedges come in steel or aluminum-bronze, which offers a softer feel for greater precision around the green. The stylish Gold version of these clubs is among the top selling specialty wedges in the game.

Finally, Callaway makes putters. No, they're not called Little Bertha's. Instead, they're called Bobby Jones Putters, after one of the greatest golfers ever to play. There are a dozen models from which to choose: From a classic look to the semi-mallet, blade-style, and heel-toe weighted versions, the Bobby Jones line offers each type of putter. The brand new BJ-11 and BJ-12 models have a deep precision-milled face with unique, long hosels.

Also from Callaway are the Carlsbad Series Putters, which come in classic shapes and are designed from stainless steel to be durable and comfortable. You can also find Tuttle putters, which have rounded soles to allow for fast, slow, Bermuda, or bent-grass greens. They are perimeter weighted and are designed to offer a great sense of club head and shaft feel. And yes, there's a Big Bertha putter—actually two of them. They are blade putters with maximum weight distribution, designed to hit the ball with smooth, consistent strokes and with less ground contact.

Cleveland Golf

Cleveland is to wedges what Callaway is to drivers, what Adams is to fairway woods, and what Ping is to putters. They have *wedged* themselves securely in the wedge market. They are, however, now offering top-quality clubs for the entire set.

Quadpro is a new line of drivers also from Cleveland that is built to give you a solid feel and exceptional distance. The *quad* comes from the combination of four metals: copper tungsten, copper, maraging steel, and stainless steel. The *pro* means you should hit like one. The low face depth is designed for you to get the ball up in the air without popping it up.

With the female golfer in mind, Cleveland Golf has designed the Emerald collection, led by multi-metal woods. The clubs handle difficult lies and are forgiving on off-center hits. The series also includes irons and wedges designed to address the needs of women golfers, which include the need for comfort, lighter weight, and ability to hit for distance at a slower swing speed.

The TA3-irons are popular with tour players because they offer precision with a compact, mid-size head featuring perimeter weighting and because they are designed for making shots from various lies. The irons also feature the Vibration Absorption System and modified v-groves, which are designed to give you proper spin and trajectory. The series includes the 1- through 9-irons plus pitching and sand wedges. You have a choice of steel or graphite shafts, and there are several flex options. The TA4 series offers larger club heads with a greater sweet spot for added power and forgiveness. Otherwise, the TA4s are similar in features to the TA3s with one additional wedge. A new series of TA5 Irons is designed for players looking for maximum forgiveness from a low-profile club. The clubs are also designed to be stable at impact and have a vibration-absorption system.

As for the top-of-the-line wedges, Cleveland Golf sports more than 30 models including sand, dual, lob, and pitch wedges ranging from 49 degrees of loft to 60. Bounce runs from 0 on the lob wedges to 14 for the sand wedges. In short, they have any type of wedge you're looking for in steel, chrome steel, beryllium nickel, or beryllium copper. The 588, 485, 691, and RTG models sport u-grooves to enhance spin so you'll be better able to stop the ball where you want it. They are also made to be nonglare and to have a sleek look and a soft feel. The nickel and copper models have a particularly soft feel for expert precision around the green.

Cleveland's Tour Action Milled Putters utilize a unique one-step milling process in which the club head and neck need not be welded together and there is no seam. This allows for a consistent, softer-feeling, one-piece putter. Four models of Tour Action Milled putters vary in features; some include heel-toe weighting and others have a longer neck. All are made to reduce twisting on off-center hits and to be easily aligned.

Along with the Tour Action Putters, Cleveland has added new Aficionado Milled Face Putters made from soft 304 steel and milled for greater tolerance. Four styles are available—named for popular cigars—and they include Portofino and Lonsdale, which each have heel-toe weighted heads;

Belicoso, featuring a slim low-profile head; and Robusto, with a larger face and double-bent shaft.

Cobra

Cobra has become one of the premier makers of both woods and irons in recent years, thanks in part to the popularity of their King Cobra line. The King Cobra Ti Titanium Offset became very popular with the "gang who couldn't shoot straight," as they helped high- and mid-handicappers control their slices. The Ti Titanium Deep Faced and oversized Deep Faced Woods were created as Cobra specialties, designed for slightly better players who know how to work the ball.

Now the folks at Cobra have introduced a whole new line, featuring Gravity Back Drivers. The shiny aluminum, bronze weight in the back of the head helps the ball get airborne easier and keeps the ball going straight. The backweight technology also helps lower the center of gravity, which increases the loft of the ball as it leaves the club. The energy transfer of this new club, coupled with an increased striking area and sweet spot, allow the ball to fly longer and straighter while also being forgiving. The club checks in with a 240cc club head and comes in both Tour and Offset models, plus the Lady Cobra Gravity Back Driver with a 235cc head and slightly higher loft angle.

Cobra's new King Cobra Baffler L.P. (low profile) fairway woods are offset with a new wider sole and a knack for hitting from difficult lies more easily thanks to their design. The low-to-the-ground profile means a lower center of gravity, which hits up on the ball while the offset club head should keep you hitting the ball straight. A 3-, 7-, and 9- are available with several choices of loft. They are designed to keep your 2-, 3-, or 4-irons in your bag.

Cobra also sports the King Cobra Titanium Fairway Woods, which add the benefits of titanium to the offset advantages, and the King Cobra Steel Fairway Woods, which have similar attributes at a little less cost.

Cobra's new Gravity Back Irons are designed to enhance performance. The backweight is now further behind the club face, and positioned to create perimeter weighting that helps the ball go further and straighter with less effort. Designed for all levels of golfer, the Gravity Back Irons are forgiving and easy to handle. They are crafted not to twist at impact. The new irons are available in one through nine, plus four wedges.

A series of Trusty Rusty Wedges are worth considering if only because of the great name. Actually, these irons, in five lofts from 53 to 61 degrees, feature soft, unplated carbon steel (that turns reddish brown and looks like it's rusted) and feature a specially designed sole that keeps you hitting the ball squarely through impact from any lie. The clubs also are designed for that desired *feel* you're looking for inside 100 yards. They also come with an instructional tape—now that's marketing!

Last, but not least, are the Bobby Grace Putters, featuring the Amazing Grace putter—in case you want to break into song—and the new Saving Grace model. The Fat Lady Swings putter also makes a return to the Cobra line after a four-year hiatus, featuring the new "smart sole design," which means you should never experience turf drag again. Additionally, other Bobby Grace putters include mallet, blade, and the popular heel-toe weighted models. Cobra calls them "the best feeling putters in the world," and says that they feature HSM (*hole-seeking material*) inserts. Marketing hype aside, they are well-crafted, smart-looking, and exceptionally soft-feeling putters designed for less drag and less twist when you hit. The Bobby Grace line is also very popular on the Senior Tour.

Daiwa

With some 30 years in the golf business and Fuzzy Zoeller representing them, Daiwa paves the way for senior golfers with the Brougham series. The Brougham G-3 driver has titanium in the head, ultra-light graphite shafts, and custom weighting to help cut down on slices and fades. Also from Daiwa is the G-3 Titanium line sporting a driver with a 270cc titanium head, bi-level sole, a super-lite surrender shaft, and an antitorque shaft design to keep the head from twisting around.

Fairway woods include the Team Daiwa Lines with titanium or titanium inserts, depending on the model, plus the oversized heads and low center of gravity for improving trajectory. The 3-, 5-, and 7-woods all come with various shaft flexes.

The latest Daiwa irons include the TD153 and TD252 for lack of better names. The 153 is a mid-size set of irons that combines the feel of a forged blade with the latest in cavity-backed head design for better weighting and forgiveness. The irons also sport an alloy center of gravity and a wider sweet spot. According to Daiwa, the 252 includes a 33 percent thicker titanium insert than most similar products to add forgiveness. The G-3 Titanium Face Line includes a stainless-steel body and solid-brass weighting at the heel and toe. The tri-metal technology sits below a super-lightweight shaft with a torquing device. The bottom line is a club designed to decrease air resistance and to allow an increased club-head speed for greater distance. Daiwa's G-3 Brougham and TD-252s come in sets of 3- through 9-irons plus pitching, flop, and sand wedges. The TD 153 and DG-201s also include the 2-iron.

Team Daiwa also makes a Driving Iron, known as the 351. The club features a low and deep center of gravity for a higher trajectory, heel-toe weighting for a more stable and forgiving club head, and a power inset on the hosel, which is where the club head meets the shaft or neck of the club.

If you can drive with an iron, why not follow it up with a fairway wood? Daiwa's special Strike Force Utility Wood has a four-rail system in the bottom to glide through any terrain. A stainless-steel club face, graphite shaft, and choice of four club face lofts round out this special *tough rough* wood.

Team Daiwa also makes the 373 CO-01 Putter. An aluminum head and a milled titanium insert give the club a softer feel. It also is heel-toe weighted. DG Milled Putters with copper/stainless steel heads and a Disc Mallet Putter also are available.

Ben Hogan

In 1954, golf legend Ben Hogan manufactured his first club called The Precision. From that point forward, the company Ben Hogan Golf was off the ground with one purpose in mind: "to build the best clubs possible." Today, the Ben Hogan line is under the larger Spalding umbrella.

Hogan does not have a line of drivers at present.

The latest innovation from the Hogan line is the 99 Apex Irons. This new line of forged irons combines the precision of forged blades with the latest enhancements from modern technology. Available in three flexes of regular, firm, and extra firm, the Apex shafts are designed to give you consistent performance and trajectory.

Special wedges also highlight the new Hogan line, featuring seven wedges that range from 52 to 60 degrees in loft and 4 to 13 in bounce. The idea is to provide the right loft and bounce so you can execute the shot you need from any distance, lie, or surface. Forged carbon steel and the popular u-grooves allow for a good feel. The Apex Forged wedges give you the opportunity to pick and choose the club that will best suit, or help, your short game.

Kunnan

In less than a decade, Kunnan has established themselves in the busy golf club making arena. They have taken a bite out of the mid to high handicappers, newer players, and seniors markets. Let's face it, that covers a lot of golfers!

Kunnan makes one-stop shopping easier with complete sets of woods, irons, and wedges plus putters that are sold separately. The EXT series features woods with a low center of gravity and an extra-light graphite shaft. These characteristics have made them very popular on the senior circuit. The EXT Ti Woods come with a super-oversize head (315cc) and a graphite crown to stabilize the club head at the point of impact. The Ti Woods are 100 percent titanium.

The EXT Irons are carefully designed to enhance performance. The shaft tip diameter, torque, and flex points vary to produce higher trajectories in the long irons and increased accuracy in the short irons. The EXT Ti Irons are muscle-backed with a pure titanium face surrounded by a stainless-steel shell for greater weight distribution and better accuracy.

The EXT 11-club set including a pitching and a sand wedge retails for under $800; the eight-piece EXT Titanium set can be had for around $650. Two other lower-priced sets for beginners are the Optima and GVS lines, both of which can get you started with clubs for under $300. (You'll spend a little more to add a putter and a bag.) Each series offers oversized clubs for more forgiveness, which is much appreciated by newer golfers. A more advanced line from Kunnan is the Tribute set, which has an oversized wood aerodynamically designed with a special sole plate to provide added club-head speed with less effort. The irons are carefully weighted and feature a sole built to reduce turf drag so you can hit more accurately from any lie.

Along with complete sets, Kunnan also offers the Mega-Bite Wedges line, wedges with lofts of 54, 60, and 62 degrees and a bounce range from 4 to 16. The wedges are beryllium copper or have either a forged copper or forged titanium insert. You also can get a Tour Grind Wedge, a soft stainless-steel wedge available in your choice of three lofts and bounces.

Kunnan putters include the Pure Putter, a heel-toe weighted model with a stainless steel insert; the Pendulum Putter, a heel-toe weighted, milled-faced putter with inserts of soft copper; and the Tribute Putter, also a heel-toe weighted putter with a soft copper insert and a steel shaft.

MacGregor Golf

Just over a century old, MacGregor currently offers several lines of irons and woods. They can furnish newer players with a complete set at a reasonable price, or they can custom-make clubs for more dedicated or advanced players.

The latest woods from MacGregor are the Tourney Tour Woods, designed for the more dedicated golfer. Oversized heads (260cc) are particularly strong, made from aerospace grade titanium. The heads are actually lighter and allow for greater forgiveness. Technically, the clubs are also designed to prevent vibration and maximize energy transfer at impact.

The DX Oversize Men's Woods (and irons) are among the most affordable quality clubs around. The stainless-steel woods feature a 240cc deep-faced driver providing maximum forgiveness. The fairway woods include shallow faces and contoured soles to reduce turf drag, and the irons are built for distance and accuracy with a low center of gravity to help you get the ball in the air. DX lines for ladies and senior models include oversized grips and are lighter for faster club-head speeds.

The latest MacGregor irons include the Tourney Forged PCB Irons and the Tourney MT Irons. The PCB's are progressive cavity-backed irons. The clubs feature a larger hitting area than most traditional forged blades with slightly larger head sizes. Also, the wider soles enhance forgiveness and make it easier to play from various lies. A progressive offset helps you get the ball in the air, while the cavity design helps you "work the club" without shifting weight— thus causing the club to hit in a direction you did not have in mind. The Tourney MT's are soft, forged-carbon steel clubs made for an outstanding feel. The longer irons have careful weight distribution and a larger hitting area.

Two series of Battlesticks woods and irons include the stainless-steel model and the Ti, or titanium, series. Both models have oversized heads and are designed to reduce turf drag while hitting more accurate shots. The irons are perimeter weighted, and the soles, or bottoms, of the clubs also are built to conform to any lie.

Other lines of woods/irons from MacGregor include the RPM, Heritage, Lady Finesse, and Battlestick Junior series.

MacGregor's new Tour Forged Wedges are precision crafted. There are two sand wedges with different lofts, a gap wedge for those "in-between" shots and a 60-degree lob wedge to get you out of deep bunkers. Tour versions of the 56 degree and 58 degree wedges are available, designed to help the finesse players "work the ball" easier. You will also still find the Reliance Series of wedges, which are cast, stainless steel, copper-insert wedges designed for enhanced feel and durability.

As is often the case, a wide assortment of putters is offered. Tourney Boralyn Putters are the latest additions. These new clubs feature boralyn—which is a patented, extremely soft, lightweight metal made from aluminum and boron carbide. Weights are added to distribute the overall weight and produce a smooth stroke. A targeted sightline is also part of the Tourney series, which comes in three models, cavity backed, mallet, and heel-toe weighted. MacGregor also offers four styles of Balata Faced Putters. These are designed with heel-toe face inserts to minimize twisting, and balata-face inserts for maximum feel and control. MacGregor Milled Face Putters are built for a truer roll, and the old-fashioned, dual-blade models send you back in golf history while giving you a durable, comfortable putter. Four models of Reliance Brass Balanced Putters have a sleek modern look with the popular heel-toe weighted cavity-back design for extra forgiveness.

MacGregor also offers Tourney forged personal irons, PMB Irons (progressive muscleback), and titanium woods all made to order. Clubs are designed to include everything from back design, sole shape, loft, lie, club length, weight, shaft, and grip. Practically any iron or wedge you desire can be made to meet your individual needs. The forged-iron heads are literally hammered, ground, and reground into shape to meet the needs of the individual player. Feel and precision are among the determining factors in designing a specially made club. The progressive muscle backs give you a more solid feel and an optimum trajectory. The titanium woods are built to be bigger and stronger yet they remain light. Insert irons, woods, and wedges also are available. The Tourney custom-made models are for the more discerning, usually low-handicap golfers who know exactly what they are looking for from their clubs.

Mizuno

Mizuno has established itself as a leader in the area of forged irons. Forging is simply a way of processing the metal so the club has a better feel and allows greater control. Naturally, when the issue is control over power, the assumption is that the clubs are for the better players. The folks at Mizuno, however, have worked long and hard to make their irons, as well as their woods, user friendly to players at all skill levels.

The new T-Zoid Pro Titanium Woods are the latest in the T-Zoid line from Mizuno. The two-piece forged-titanium club head is designed for distance and optimum control. The Pro Titanium has a grain-flow, forged-titanium face and neck to give you a softer feel with a maximum energy transfer for increased distance. The Pro models are custom fit. The Mighty Big Titanium Driver, meanwhile, has an extra-large club head and sports a unique sole design. Like other T-Zoids, it has Mizuno's Active Kick design for more *kick* at impact.

The new T-Zoid Comp EZ Iron is oversized, allowing for a greater sweet spot from which to strike the ball. The clubs feature the cavity-back design to distribute weight more optimally and to allow for greater consistency and more forgiveness for mid to high handicappers. The new line of EZ irons also has a low center of gravity for getting the ball into the air.

The T-Zoid Sure Cast Irons also are an oversized lot; they're made of steel and are wider across the bottom. Combining the width with a lower center of gravity, the new club has a larger sweet spot. The Sure series also has a graphite shaft with Mizuno's Active Kick technology. The Sure irons come with steel or graphite shafts. Custom fitting in select golf specialty stores gives golfers the sure fit with this line of T-Zoid cast irons.

The new EZ and T-Zoid Sure irons follow the success of the T-Zoid Pro Forged Irons, which followed the MP-14 line that became very popular on the PGA Tour. The MP-14 irons are nickel-chrome–plated and designed for feel and control while reducing turf drag. A 3- through pitching wedge are included in the set, and the 1- and 2-irons and sand wedge are available separately.

Odyssey

Even though they're putter specialists, Odyssey also makes clubs to help you get onto the green. The Dual Force Wedges feature light faces that accentuate perimeter weighting and that help you hit accurately while providing forgiveness when necessary. A special vibration-dampening material enhances the feel in the line of three wedges that check in at lofts of 52, 56, and 60 degrees.

Now for the main course: Odyssey putters are the cream of the crop. The Rossie 2—used by Nick Faldo and other pros on the various tours—is a mallet with a soft feel and superb face balance. It can be yours with a choice of either a steel or bronze head. The secret to Odyssey's super-soft impact is something called *stronomic*, a new space-age material that provides a gentle feel while giving you greater consistency. Dual Force uses a combination of stronomic and more widely used metals to create the popular line. The recently unveiled Triforce 1 and Triforce 2 putters offer three materials—stainless steel, tungsten and Stronomic elastomer. Rapidly becoming as popular as the Dual Force models, the Triforce putters reposition weight in the head of the putter for improved feel and performance.

Dual Force Odyssey mallet putters include the Rossie 1, Rossie 2, Deep Face Rossie 2, Dual Force Rossie 2 Bronze, and 330 Mallet. Much of the difference is in the look of the putter and the visual setup, plus, of course, the feel and comfort level. All are designed for a smooth, comfortable stroke and a gentle feel when meeting the ball.

The Rossie Blade has the same features as the mallet but in a traditional blade style; the face-balanced Rossie FV1 adds more perimeter weighting and features a double S-bend steel shaft. There also are Rossie Long Putters for people who like an extra tall putter at 46, 48, or 50 inches. A wide variety of models offer easy alignments, heel-toe weighting, stronomic inserts, blade models, and a soft feel for each putting preference.

Orlimar

If Orlimar sounds like the name of the latest heavy metal band, it's appropriate. The gang at Orlimar is the self proclaimed leader in multimetal technology. Their latest TriMetal series is gaining a lot of attention.

Orlimar's TriMetal technology has produced a club face that's 85 percent harder than pure titanium. The weight is carefully distributed thanks to three copper-tungsten inlays. The combination of metals and careful weighting helps put the ball in the air with greater accuracy and distance. The driver, with a midsize face (200cc), comes in three lofts with ultra-light graphite shafts featuring a lower balance point to increase the trajectory. It also has a larger tip diameter to increase feel and to give you better stability on off-center hits.

The TriMetal Fairway Woods come in nine lofts from 9 degrees up to 27. They feature the *Alpha metal maraging* or metal technology of the woods including stainless-steel shells and copper-tungsten weights in the sole plate. This gives the club a low center of gravity for desired trajectory and improved accuracy. The fairway woods as well as the driver come in five flexes.

Orlimar's TriMetal Irons are longer and are designed for
the optimum trajectory for each club face and loft. The
Low Profile Long Irons have a low center of gravity to get
the ball airborne more easily. Also available are the Compact Mid Irons and the Traditional Short Irons. The three
types of irons differ in their placement of the copper-
tungsten inlay for differing results. Golfers can match the
irons to the characteristics of their game. They also feature
ultra-light graphite shafts.

Ping

When golfers think of Ping, they think of top-quality
irons and putters. Ping introduced the idea of perimeter
weighting and has been the leader in customizing clubs
for players at all levels.

Not wanting to be left out, they introduced a titanium
driver, the ISI, that has generated a great deal of attention.
Sporting a 300cc club head, the ISI Titanium also is designed in a unique manner with a flatter top for less dis-
tortion on your approach and when striking the ball. The
club head is built to provide better energy transfer, which
means you'll hit the ball farther. A weight in the back of
the club face helps keep the club stable during impact for
straighter shots. It also makes it less likely that you'll twist
the club on your swing and allows for more forgiveness if
you somehow still manage to miss-hit the ball. Club specifications are made to order, giving you a number of
choices so the club will best suit your needs. You choose
the loft, shaft, hosel, and flex of the club.

Ping's ISI Tour Woods offer the 1-, 3-, 5-, 7-, and 9- and
feature an innovative design that replaces the weight in
the center of the club with an insert as a form of perimeter weighting. The light insert should enhance the club
and should give you a softer *wood* feel for greater control
and forgiveness.

The ISI Irons are among the top sellers in the game. Careful weight distribution to avoid twisting on off-center hits

(thus making them very forgiving) is the secret to much of the ISI iron's popularity. Lower-handicap golfers, however, also like the feel because they are better able to work the ball. A wider sole on the club also allows you to hit more easily from various lies. The ISI-K line has an oversized steel-blade club face and a larger sweet spot, which appeals to the average golfer. The ISI-Nickel, Copper, and S series offer a greater feel for lower-handicap players and allow players to better work the ball. Nickel, though tougher, provides a softer feel; copper, a denser material, allows for the weighting to be distributed in four locations around the club head. The ISI follows the lines of EYE2 and Zing2 irons, which helped make Ping a major player in the industry in recent years. The Eye2 has been a proven favorite with tour players, producing more than 250 wins worldwide. Apparently the eyes have it!

ISI Wedges come in six lofts from 47 to 61 and are offered in copper, nickel, or the more common stainless steel. Ping customizing allows you to select from 24 possible choices including loft, lie, and bounce. It's almost like a wedge salad bar.

And where would the game be without Ping putters? The latest innovation in Ping putters is called Isopur. What is Isopur, you ask? It's a material designed to make the club feel particularly soft once it's poured onto the face of the putter. Isopur notwithstanding, Ping putters feature the perimeter weighting that has made them famous, as well as sharp image lines. The Ping Zing 2i (talk about great names) has an extremely soft touch and is a very easy putter to align. The Nellie is a mallet with heel-toe weighting to make it easy on any surface and for any putting style. The Bergan is a neat-looking putter made of bronze and aluminum with heel-toe weighting to resist twisting. The Faith has Isopur in a bronze shell. It's face-balanced with a center of gravity away from the club face so that the ball rotates faster and moves more smoothly. It has a unique look, too. Other Ping putters include the B60I, Anser series, BZ series, Sedona, B90I, Pal series, Darby, and Scottsdale to name a few. In short, Ping can furnish you with whatever putter will work best for you on the green.

Taylor Made

One of the premier club manufacturers around today, Taylor Made has built its reputation, in part, with its Bubble Metalwoods and Bubble Burner Irons. Taylor made is now building on that foundation with their new Firesole line of clubs.

The new Firesole Woods are designed to place the right weight in the places, where you need it most for maximum distance and accurate shots. The goal is to provide you with more impact at less swing speed. The Firesoles incorporate tungsten and titanium plugs under and behind where you hit the ball. Locating the proper center of gravity for maximum effectiveness, the club is designed to generate tremendous power at impact. Some marketing power will come from Mark O'Meara. The Masters and British Open winner started using Firesole Woods shortly after they were introduced.

The Ti Bubble 2 is the second generation of the Bubble series. A popular over-faced driver, the new 2 sports a 20-percent bigger club head and is remarkably lighter than its predecessor. It also allows for faster club-head speeds, which have been clocked at an average of 155 mph off the face. Improvements in the face of the titanium club head also have added a more boring, flatter trajectory, which makes shots longer and gives you greater roll. The oversized heads on the Ti Bubble 2 Fairway Woods (from 3- to 7-woods) are easy to hit with and are very forgiving. A low center of gravity coupled with the unique club design allow for comfortable hitting off all kinds of lies. Several flexes are offered, and lofts range from 7.5 to 11.5. For better golfers, or lower handicappers, the Tour Forged Ti Bubble 2 has a smaller head and a more concentrated sweet spot. This is for the golfer looking for more precision and control who is less concerned about forgiveness. (Hence, it's for someone who does not miss-hit the ball often.)

Firesole Rescue Clubs are a new hybrid that falls somewhere between a wood and an iron. A low profile iron with a fairway wood body, the clubs are designed to provide the accuracy of an iron and the power of a wood to "rescue you" on that all too challenging second shot. Putting 75 percent of the weight below the ball, these Rescue Clubs will help put any shot into the air, while solving the age-old problem of weather or not to hit with a wood or an iron. The Tungsten/Titanium clubs come in four lofts and are built to balance power and control while building confidence.

For the shot following your "rescue," Taylor Made has both Firesole and Ti Bubble 2 irons, depending where you shop. The new Firesole Series of irons ranges from a 3-iron to a pitching wedge—all made from titanium and tungsten and featuring generous sweet spots. The clubs are long irons that are easy to handle, thus hitting like short irons. Taylor Made bills them not as a series, but as a "team of irons"; which mean either they huddle in your bag rather than just sit there, or that they compliment each other as distinct clubs, each with a job to do.

Ti Bubble 2 Irons have the oversized titanium head that puts 80 percent of the club's weight under the ball at impact, lifting it up. The club is fully heel-toe weighted so you get more stability with your power as the ball gets airborne. Taylor Made calls the combination "feel, forgiveness, and flight." The Burner LCG (Lower Center of Gravity) Irons also give you more weight, and therefore power, below the center of the ball. Burner Tour Irons, like the Tour Woods, are designed more for precision than power and are played by a number of pros. The Champaigne Burner LCG Irons are the women's version of the previously mentioned clubs with smaller grips and an ultra-light Bubble 2 shaft for increased power.

The Taylor Made Tour Wedge series of four clubs ranges from 50 to 61 degrees in loft and 3 to 12 in bounce. U-shaped grooves give you enhanced backspin to keep the ball on the green, and constant friction inserts are included to add better spin and an enhanced softer feel to put the ball where you want it ... *on the green (near the pin).*

Two types of putters include the Burner NCs and the Roho Putters. The Burner NCs are a series of five putters, each weighted to compliment different stroke tendencies with different balancing. The idea is to give you the putter that counterbalances whatever it is you do to consistently miss putts, whether you hit to the left, hit to the right, or push or pull your putts. The Roho putters are defined by Taylor Made as "solid and soft, steady and smooth, and steady and straight." In quarter-, half-, or full-mallet design, they also look *sleek and striking* with copper heads plus aluminum in the body and face. The copper and aluminum combo gives these putters a soft, light-weight feel plus better distance control on longer putts.

TearDrop

Masters of the putt, the gang at TearDrop offers what they call Roll-Face technology, which is designed to enhance consistency and control on the green by giving you more consistent impact with less skid. Striking the ball below the midpoint, or equator, gives you better control and a more pure roll.

Among the putters from TearDrop are the TD00 and the TD21. The TD00 is a heel-toe weighted model that's face-balanced with a single-bend shaft for maximum feel and control—plus, of course, the Roll-Face technology. The TD21 also is heel-toe weighted with a short-length blade and a straight shaft. Most of the line has the classic TearDrop logo, and all models can be had in 33, 34, 35, or 36 inches. The feel and consistency of the TearDrop line of putters have made them extremely popular.

Titleist

From the golf ball kings come the Titleist Titanium drivers, which already have seen tour victories at the Kemper Open and the PGA Championship. The clubs are carefully weighted to provide a solid feel plus precision. The center of gravity is positioned higher and closer to the heel. The 975D is a large, deep-faced, pear-shaped driver with an oversized 260cc head; the 976R has a slightly smaller round head (210cc) with a more shallow face. The 976R is designed for the golfer seeking shot workability and trajectory control—in other words, the better players. The new titanium drivers also are designed for maximum energy transfer at impact for more solid shots. Graphite shafts are lightweight to counterbalance the titanium heads and come in your choice of flexes. Women's and senior versions also are available.

Following the success of their popular Titanium 975 driver, the gang at Titleist have introduced their new Pro Trajectory 975F Fairway Metals. The club has a long hosel designed to distribute weight toward the heel for better trajectory and shot control. A deeper center of gravity will help get the ball airborne without much difficulty. Balanced weight also reduces spin. The combination should provide flatter, higher shots. Designed with the more serious golfer in mind, the new Fairway Metals come in three trajectories with a choice of shafts including gold steel and three types of graphite.

Titleist's DCI Irons are a top-of-the-line series for serious golfers. The clubs are carefully crafted to enhance precise shot-making, and they are weighted to counteract miss-hits. Along the sole, a patented Triple Grind glides more smoothly through the turf and helps you maintain club-head speed through impact. Two lines of clubs, the DCI962 and DCI981, come in 1- through 9-woods and offer four wedges. The DCI981SL series is made for players with a slower swing speed. Both lines of DCI81s are made with contemporary blades cast from 431 stainless steel with a rear cavity weight shelf to provide enhanced feel and performance. The DCI962 Oversized line is 15 percent larger than the traditional 962's and provides a greater resistance to twisting. A moderate offset helps players work their shots with right-to-left or left-to-right action.

Vokey Wedges are the latest in wedge technology and are named for Titleist's Senior Product Engineer Bob Vokey. The series of seven wedges is offered in three classic profiles and is designed for the more discerning players. Cast from carbon steel to provide ultimate feel, the wedges feature U-grooves for maximum spin and control and allow you to select the loft, shape, sole, and bounce combination you want. A specialty gap wedge, a sand wedge, a true sand wedge for firmer conditions, a lob wedge, a versatile lob wedge for escaping the deep grass or sand, a classic 60s-style wedge, and a tour wedge round out an impressive line from Vokey and Titleist.

Milled from a solid block of soft carbon steel, Cameron Teryllium putters have been known to provide enhanced feel. An inlay of teryllium in the face is part of the secret formula for producing the soft feel in a solid, well-crafted club. Thus, the new Cameron Teryllium II line is designed to be even that much softer with insert technology enhancing the feel. The Santa Fe Two and Del Mar Two Long Slant are among several of the popular series that have been refined. The latest features include multi material construction complete with teryllium inlays and precision craftsmanship that dampen vibration at impact while smoothly striking the ball. In addition, a new Cameron Pro Platinum line offers a further choice of feel with four models including the Del Mar Three, Laguna Two, Newport Mid Slant and Sonoma Two. The new series has a choice of slant neck or flare neck for golfers who like different appearances at the set-up position.

A wide variety of putters that are already part of the Titleist line are the popular Newport Series with long neck models, classic designs with an L-neck, heel-toe weighted designs with a semi-rounded sight line, longer head single sight line models and so on. Cameron putters are built to provide the right feel for you, and since no two golfers are alike, they make a wide range of models.

Top Flite

From the golf ball kings at Spalding come some very well-received clubs sporting the latest technology and old-fashioned comfort and control.

The Intimidator Titanium 400 Woods already have made their mark on the Senior PGA circuit. A larger tip is designed to maintain stability so the club is less likely to twist during impact. A titanium-cast head provides maximum power, and the shaft is light for increased club-head speed. The club also has a thicker section in the middle that is designed to provide trajectory control.

The 400 Fairway Woods have a low center of gravity to help get the ball airborne. A Spoiler sole is designed to get the ball out of any lie. The woods come in 3-, 5-, 7-, and 9- and with a variety of flex options.

Top Flite also offers Tour Irons with oversized, cavity-backed heads for balance and greater forgiveness on off-center hits. A bar located behind the sweet spot enhances distance and provides a more solid feel when striking the ball. Muscle graphite shafts are engineered to flex in the proper place for the right trajectory. The Tour Oversized line provides even more club face so you can't possibly not meet the ball from any lie. The Tour Titanium models are steel with a hard titanium face. The combination provides maximum perimeter weighting for greater stability.

Also from Top Flite comes a brand new series of Tour Wedges. The new series includes approach, sand, utility, and lob wedges, which continue in the popular line of irons. A longer hosel changes the balance of the club head, shifting more weight toward the heel and higher up on the face. This allows players to gain a better degree of precision and control. The cover coating of the wedges has been carefully coated with a blend of tungsten and nickel, which enhances the feel and protects the surface to help maintain the club. V-shaped grooves allow the clubs to glide smoothly through any lie. The models come in 52, 56, 58, and 60 degrees of loft with bounce ranging from 4 for the lob to 12 for the sand wedge. The new Tour Wedges already are being played on all the major tours.

Wilson

Wilson makes a wide variety of clubs and offers complete sets for your one-stop shopping needs. Their emphasis remains on making the avid average golfer play better. With that in mind, their newest driver is the Fat Shaft Ti Super Oversize Driver. As the name would imply, the shaft is fatter. This gives you more stability while making it less likely that you'll twist the club when swinging. Combined with the titanium club face, the Fat Shaft Driver offers you longer shots, maximum stability, and a large sweet spot for more forgiveness. The club comes in four flexes and several loft choices and has three fairway woods (3-, 5-, and 7-) following in its path. The fairway woods have *railer sole designs*, which basically means you can get the club face through the grass more easily. A lower center of gravity helps you get under the ball to get it in the air.

A major sporting good manufacturer, Wilson has clubs for all levels of golfers. The Pro Staff series includes the new Wide Tip line featuring an oversized stainless-steel head for increased durability, feel, and control plus a larger sweet spot for miss-hits. Wider, lightweight graphite shafts give you longer, straighter hits due to club-head stability and allow for increased club-head speed for longer shots. The 1200 Tour Woods also sport an oversized head plus a *drop-away sole*, which improves aerodynamics and resists turf drag. These clubs also feature stainless-steel heads and graphite shafts designed to dampen vibration so you can swing more easily through impact. The Ultra Tour and OS (oversized) lines also are popular. The Tour model includes titanium inserts for increased distance and feel, and the oversize models are perimeter weighted cast-iron drivers with aluminum heads and graphite reflex shafts designed to increase club-head speed.

Among the other Wilson lines of clubs are the 1200 Ti titanium series of drivers and fairway woods and the Killer Whale series with titanium face inserts.

The latest irons, the Fat Shaft Irons, are cast oversize irons. Each one has a fatter shaft to handle the club face with more stability. The clubs are designed to glide through the grass so you will hit the ball squarely. Easy alignments and the large face make miss-hits less likely but forgiving should you not hit the ball as you'd like. The Fat Shaft Tour series include the Tour Cast and the RM Tour, designed for precision and accuracy. The Tour Cast models are cavity back perimeter weighted clubs with a midsize head and easy alignment for setting up your shot. Both lines come with a choice of flex.

The latest Wilson Wedges are also Fat Shafts including the Aluminum Bronze Sand Wedge and the Dyna-Powered Wedges. The Aluminum Bronze has a softer feel than stainless steel, which, along with the Fat Shaft, provides a more solid feel and greater control. Loft angle on this sand wedge is 57 degrees. The Dyna-Powered Wedges have won the favor of tour players. They are a series of forged carbon steel clubs including a gap wedge at 52 degree loft, a sand wedge at 56, and a loft wedge at 60, with appropriate bounces for different surfaces.

A host of putters include the Fat Shaft Copper series of seven putters for every need including heel-toe weighting and a choice of blade or mallet style. The copper inserts are designed to generate a better, smoother feel. Traditional classic putters offer a special leather wrap on your grip if you so desire. For lack of more interesting names, the 8802, 8813, and 8806 are classic putters with flared-out backs for balance and control and forged carbon steel for a soft feel. Other clubs include an array of Black Jack extra-soft-feeling balata putters in various shapes and styles, the Ultra putters with oversized heads, the classic shiny-gold Augusta putter (which might be as close as you'll ever get to playing the Augusta course), and various Alignment putters to suit every man, woman, and child who wants to try the game.

Wilson also offers complete club packages, sometimes referred to as starter sets. The Advantage and Matrix packages come complete with woods, irons, wedges, a putter, and a bag. Both are quality packages designed to help beginning golfers get the ball in the air. They have larger sweet spots and shafts designed for a comfortable feel and to enhance a smooth swing. In short, Wilson wants you to enjoy the game and to get started with a comfortable, not pricey set of clubs.

Popular Junior Sets include the Michael Jordan Junior Package with an oversized 1-wood, flexible oversized 5-, 7-, and 9-irons, and a putter. The Jordan set includes a lightweight golf bag but no basketball. The Pro Staff Extreme Junior Set includes a wood, 5-, 7-, and 9-irons, a putter, and a lightweight bag. The 36-inch wood is oversized, and the clubs have graphite wood shafts designed for junior players. Both are excellent choices for young golfers who are just learning the game.

Zevo

The Zevo custom club designers are dedicated to fitting each golfer with the club best suited for his or her game. A smorgasbord of club parts, Zevo lets you determine the lie angles, lofts, offset for irons, wood head design, iron head design, shaft type, flex, grips, and more. They are very accommodating.

The Air Zero Oversized Metalwoods have a longer, narrower face with a lower center of gravity for optimum trajectory. The Comp Equipe models are designed for the player looking to work the ball with greater precision. The new Zevo Fly-Ti features lightweight, high-energy titanium heads.

Air Zevo Fairway Woods include the 2-, 3-, and 5-irons with the 3- and 5- coming in your choice of loft angles. The Comp Equipe line features a higher center of gravity, and the oversized models have a lower center of gravity and large club head designed for maximum launch and a higher ball flight. The Fly-Ti Fairway Insert Metal Woods are configured to handle any lie or face angle requirements. They are custom-fitted metal woods available in Competition and Low Profile models.

Irons include the new Zevo Blades designed for the low to mid handicapper. Made from soft carbon molybdenum (called Copper Molly by the gang at Zevo), these irons have a softer feel at impact and are designed to help with fine precision. The club is offset with a longer face and a wider sole than previous Zevo entries. The low-profile Fly-Ti Irons are stainless steel with titanium inserts. The inserts place more weight in the sole of the club and produce a lower center of gravity. Zevo irons, like the drivers and fairway woods, are custom fitted for lie angle, shaft length, shaft flex, and grip size.

Others

Other companies making clubs include Alien, Carbite, Tommy Armour, Black Ice, Dunlop, Izzo, Maxfli, Nicklaus, Gary Player, Powerbilt, Ram, Slazenger, Wood Brothers, and Yonex.

Chapter 3

Golf Bags

Once you have clubs, golf balls, and various other minor accouterments such as a towel and rain gear, you'll obviously need something in which to carry it all around—hence, the golf bag. Unlike handbags, they need not match your shoes.

Several varieties of bags are designed to suit your needs. Bags you carry will be lighter and usually will have fewer pockets for "stuff" than the bigger bags that sit on the back of your cart. Some models offer the best of both worlds; they're light enough to carry without Monday morning backaches, but they have enough pockets for accessories. Although carry bags are designed to be durable and to keep your clubs in a comfortable setting, it's important from your perspective for the shoulder strap (or straps) to be padded and comfortable.

Essentially, a golf bag should

- Hold clubs, balls, and other essentials without bouncing them around too much as you walk or ride.

- Be light enough to carry comfortably for 18 holes if you do not use a cart.

- Be made of durable material that will survive inclement weather and the trunk of your car.

- Have the look you desire.

- Provide easy access to everything you need from a variety of easily accessible pockets.

Beyond that, the various options are just a matter of personal preference. It's not unlike the comfort and convenience of sitting in your car and having drink holders and other luxuries that make life on the road—or, in this case, on the course—easier. Some golfers like many hidden, zipped-up pockets; others complain that they can't find what they need if there are too many compartments. Bags often have anywhere from 5 to 15 pockets. As for colors, pick the one that suits you. Darker colors tend to show less dirt. How many dividers you need might depend on how much you paid for each club and how much you want to separate the clubs you like from those you hate. Full-length dividers can be beneficial to the shafts so they won't clank around. Many bags offer *graphite shaft protection*.

One option that has gained a lot of attention and that has merit is the standing bag for people who carry their clubs. These bags have legs like a tripod (except only two) that keep the bag standing so it doesn't get wet from the ground and so your clubs and balls don't fall out every time you lay it down. Standing bags also benefit your back because you don't need to bend over time and time again to pick up the bag or to pull out a different club.

Bags generally range in price from the $50 basic, lightweight bag for carrying a few clubs to the larger, more durable $500 cart bag that you can practically climb inside when it starts to rain. Like everything else, the more options and the finer the materials used to make the bag, the higher the price.

When shopping for a bag, make sure you take some time to walk around wearing it. Put clubs in it and see how it feels. If it feels heavy for five minutes in the store, you'll be in big trouble carrying it for 18 holes on the course. Make sure the strap feels comfortable on your shoulder and is not digging into your skin. Some companies now utilize the X-strap created by Sun Mountain or the dual-strap systems from Izzo to take the weight off one shoulder. This provides better balance and weight distribution. You can be sure the marketing department of some golf-equipment manufacturer will start calling it *back perimeter weighting* if they haven't already.

Another back-saver to look for is handles or grips that help you pull the heavier bags out of the trunk of your car.

Bag size generally is measured by the diameter across the top. The larger cart bags are 10 or 11 inches in diameter, and the smaller ones are around 7 inches in diameter. Weight and size of the overall bag will be comparable to each other. Some golf bags actually are as light as 3–4 pounds (before you load them up). Bags are further divided into anywhere from 2 to 14 compartments into which to slide clubs. Many players are satisfied keeping woods, irons, and wedges in three sections and the putter in an extra putter pocket. It's a matter or personal preference.

The following sections discuss the myriad of golf bags from which you can choose.

Bennington

Since 1987 the California company, specializing in golf bags, has been putting out new lines annually. They continue to grow in size and scope, now reaching a world-wide market.

> **Stellar Grid & Organizer Bag.** Okay, so the name stinks, but this $9^1/_2$-inch bag is well crafted with a

14-grid sponge foam organizer insert and a putter holder (or a scabbard as they call it). A two-level hood snaps to accommodate longer woods, and all pockets have front access so you won't have to circle your bag to get what you need. The bag is durable and, thanks to waterproof dynalon, keeps your clubs dry.

Pilot and Swift X Bags. At last, bags for *X-Files* fans. The Pilot features full-length cloth dividers to protect your graphite shafts and has six pockets, a rain hood, and a stable stand. The Swift X is a light $3^1/_2$ pounds and includes most of the same features. Both sport the X-strap for easy carrying and for less strain on one shoulder.

Ladies Pouch Classic Tapestry Bag. Complete with optional matching head covers and a shoe bag for the lady who likes to accessorize on the course, Bennington offers this 9-inch cart bag with their new 14-hole grid organizer. A large double-zippered, wide-opening ball pocket plus two large pouch pockets and a *magic tape* glove attachment highlight this ladies' model.

Walker Lite Stand Bag. A lightweight carrying bag with the dual-strap system for carrying comfort, the Walker Lite has automatically retracting legs and four-way dividers with a fur-lined top. A mesh pouch, a mesh pocket, and a detachable-apparel pouch also are on board.

Bridgestone

Bridgestone, the Georgia based long time makers of golf balls, moved into the bag business in more recent years as part of their ongoing growth in the industry. They feature several standing bags, some of which are self standing and others with the now popular retractable stand.

Tour Bag. Used by touring pros, this model is part of Bridgestone's popular Precept golf line and comes in either 9- or 10-inch varieties. It has a six-way divided top (three full length) along with ample pocket space and a matching rain or travel hood.

Stand Bags. Featuring an easy-to-open-and-close, two-position stand, the durable line of Precept Stand Bags includes three-way full-length dividers, a matching rain or travel hood, and dual-strap adaptability in a lightweight bag. Enhancing these 8^1/$_2$-inch models is a zip-away compartment that makes the bag easily adaptable for carts, if necessary, or for travel or storage.

Burton

Burton began in 1907 as a maker of handcrafted horse collars and harnesses. By 1923 they were in the golf bag business which is where they remained among the leaders for the rest of the decade. Although they have advanced from hand made goods to a factory with state of the art manufacturing equipment, they still carefully hand check and put their products through numerous tests to assure their quality.

Premier, Premier Pinehurst, and Premier Signature. Burton offers leather, 10-inch diameter bags with a six-way top, five pockets, and a zippered hood on their Pinehurst cart models. The 9^1/$_2$-inch, four-pocket, leather/twill combination Signature series also is a big seller. The traditional Premier line consists of 10-inch bags made from deluxe suede. Each line of bags comes with a lifetime warrantee from Burton.

Destin. More than a dozen models of the traditional-style Destin and Destin Deluxe golf bags are available. The twill suede or twill vinyl line feature a

9-inch diameter bag with four pockets, graphite
protection, and zippered hoods. The Lady Destin
series features elegant tapestries and other hand-
woven materials for a sophisticated look.

Classic Lite. A light polyester/vinyl bag, the Classic
Lite and Lady Classic Lite are 8¹/₂ inches in diameter,
have three pockets, have zippered hoods, and are
obviously much lighter weight than the Destins.

Hiker. A 9-inch carry bag with dual straps, the Hiker
is lightweight with plenty of features. Nine pockets,
graphite protection, and a zippered hood highlight
these polyester/suede bags that come in more than
half a dozen models.

Burton bags also include The Expeditions, which are lightweight (how lightweight depends on what you stuff into
the pockets) with 15 pockets plus tube construction for a
high-tech look. Also offered are the cart and carry combo
bags in the Z and Viper lines. In addition, Burton makes a
PGA Tour and President's Cup line of monogrammed bags
that range from tour staff to lightweight carry and stand
bags. Corporate or collegiate bags with your company
logo or school letters also are offered. In short, Burton will
custom design any bag you like made to order.

Burton also offers the new Niblock security system, which
can be yours in most models for a little bit extra. The system has a shifting divider plate that can secure the club
compartment and a built-in retractable cable to tie your
clubs and bag to a fixed object.

Callaway

Callaway, famous for the Big Berthas, have been in the
bag business since the late 80's. They do not actually
manufacture bags, but market and sell bags made by ven-
dors for Callaway.

Staff Series Bags. These three models of cart bags sport the famous Callaway and Big Bertha logos. The $10^1/_2$, $9^1/_2$ and Mini Staff Bags feature six-way divided tops, durable vinyl material, tube construction, full-length shaft dividers to protect your clubs, and a zippered travel or rain hood.

Ultra-Lite Stand Bags. This popular Callaway series includes the X-Strap technology for back comfort developed by Sun Mountain Sports and the dual strap developed by Izzo Systems. In addition to the easier, more comfortable carrying features, the stand bags include $8^1/_2$-inch, four-way divided tops, roller bottoms with retractable stands, and roomy pockets (including a mesh pocket).

Callaway also features the Sir Isaac's line, sturdy Medallion Stand Bags, and the sleek Ladies Gem line.

Cobra

Just as they work long and hard to create state of the art clubs, Cobra carefully engineers golf bags designed to be both functional and have a sleek look. They constantly upgrade bags to include the latest features.

Tour Staff and Color Staff. The Tour Staff has a six-way, fur-lined top with full-length club dividers, a large belly pocket, a ball pocket, and a matching rain hood. The new Color Staff series has similar features plus a valuables pouch and a shoe compartment. Both are cart bags. A new, slightly smaller and less expensive Outback model also is offered from Cobra.

Airstand and Sunday Stand. Only 5 and 3 pounds respectively, these stand bags are lightweight and durable. They have padding for comfort while carrying them, dual-ball pockets, valuables pockets, and easy-to-open stands to keep them off the ground while you're swinging away.

Cobra also makes travel covers and mesh shoe bags for when you hit the road.

Gregory Paul

Makers of golf and duffle bags, the New York based company features first rate stand and cart bags. They are also one of the foremost designers of bags with country club logos found in the top clubs nationwide.

> **The Classic Stand Bag.** The Classic is a $9^{1}/_{2}$-inch bag weighing in at under 6 pounds. The bag has two full-length dividers, nine pockets, a hood with a two-way zipper, plus legs that are sturdy and easily retractable.

> **The New Classic.** A solid cart bag, The New Classic has two dividers, five pockets, and a putter holder.

Also from bag-making specialist Gregory Paul are the Balliwick, a large cart bag with a six-way top and a long clothing pocket; the light, oval Carnoystie, a $7^{1}/_{2}$-inch diameter bag with enough room for the essentials at a lower price; and the popular Adirondack, a bag with two full-length cushioned dividers and four pockets on a sharp-looking, tan, synthetic-leather-trimmed durable bag.

Ben Hogan

The Ben Hogan Company has enjoyed ongoing success since they began in the early 1950's with their first golf clubs. They advanced to popular golf balls in the 1970's and 80's and on to golf bags which have met the needs of touring professionals in the 1990's.

> **Staff Bags.** From Ben Hogan and the gang at Spalding come the cream of the crop. Eleven inches in diameter, the Staff Bag, which retails for $600—along with it's $9^{1}/_{2}$-inch younger sibling at $500—are carefully designed with a three-point harness to

enhance weight distribution. Sporting the Ben Hogan logo, the bags have seven large pockets and a comfortable padded strap.

Stand Bags. Featuring a double-sling design with special cushioning to be gentler and kinder to your shoulders, this carry/stand bag is lightweight yet highly functional with ample pockets. The easy-to-open stand balances the bag on all sorts of terrain.

Classic Bags. A great deal (retailing for a third the cost of the Staff Bag), the Classic has eight pockets (including a shoe pocket) in a durable 9-inch, fur-lined, well-crafted bag.

Jones

Specialists in the area of golf bags, the designers at Jones Sports Company try to combine functionality with durability and make bags that will last. They are very popular with the golfing college crowd, including alumni, as they are licensed to sell items with logos from a vast number of schools and universities.

Step Up. The golf bag veterans at Jones Sporting Goods Company offer a series of durable, lightweight, well-balanced bags. The Step Up model features two full-length dividers, eight easily accessible pockets, and padded, comfortable shoulder straps in one of several materials and in a choice of 225 solid colors or any two-color combination.

Packer. The Packer series includes the Packer Step Up, which includes the features of the Step Up model plus an enlarged pocket for clothes and a ball pocket for a total of 10 pockets. A clear, waterproof rain hood, fur-lined dividers, an umbrella holder, and an optional dual-strap system for comfortable carrying also are part of the Packer Step Up. The model also has a patented leg system sporting a lifetime guarantee. The Packers come in 9- or 7³/₄-inch diameter sizes. Packer Carry and Junior models also are available.

Super Deluxe. The Jones Super Deluxe series includes several styles of 9- and 10-inch diameter bags. The top-of-the-line bags (complete with saddle bags) are all-vinyl and feature large pockets with zippered mesh for wet clothes; a double-belted, fur-lined top; a waterproof tube liner; umbrella holders; detachable, padded shoulder straps; a rain hood; and a handy trunk grip. Styles include beautifully embroidered designs as well as models in polyduck with vinyl trim or in solid vinyl.

Jones also makes high-quality, padded, airline-travel covers with or without pockets.

MacGregor Golf

The 102 year old company makes a wide range of bags (around 135 different bags to be more precise) sold globally. MacGregor was proud to be the first company to make golf bags for women, starting in the 1950's with a bag popularized by Louise Suggs, a champion in her day.

DX. The DX Cart Bag is a durable model with an inner lining and a special handle for pulling it out of the car. A four-way top with full-length dividers plus 10, count 'em 10, pockets provides room to store everything from shoes to nuts. The bag also includes a rain/travel hood, a towel ring, and an umbrella holder. The DX Deluxe Cart Bag has even more! Added features include a detachable pouch, a cellular-phone holder, an umbrella sleeve, and five more pockets so you won't have to leave anything at home. For people who carry their bags, the lighter DX Stand Bag is a tough, polyester bag with steel-stay construction that weighs in at 5 pounds. A four-sectioned pocket stores your jacket while a valuable pocket stores valuables or hides your scorecard. An umbrella stand with a lock and an easy-to-open stand round out the light yet sturdy bag.

Flip Bags. The Flip Organizer Bag provides 14 sections with full-length graphite protection, giving each club a home of it's own. Nine inches in diameter, the cart bag includes eight pockets, a sturdy inner lining, an umbrella well and tee holders, a water-resistant zippered hood, an adjustable foam-molded sling for comfortable carrying from your car, and a bottom assist handle for getting the bag from your trunk. The Flip Stand Organizer Bags include the same 14 sections but are lighter, have four pockets, and are designed for carrying. They also have the easy-to-operate, sturdy stand.

MacGregor also makes Xtra Lite and Aerolite Stand Bags with dual-zippered pockets in lightweight, easy-to-carry designs. Most MacGregor bags come in a few models sporting different looks and colors.

Mizuno

Mizuno began making golf bags at the start of the 90's. An international company, they have an exclusive line of bags designed for North America, which is updated with new features annually. The bags are designed to be practical, durable and resistant to the elements.

Omega. The Omega LX series contains distinctive, high-quality bags that are 10 inches in diameter and have six-way, fully padded departments and an external slot for the putter. A specially lined jewelry pocket, an insulated beverage pocket, and a cellular-phone pocket are among the additional features. The LX series come in five styles. The Omega cart bag is a slightly heavier yet similarly designed bag with most of the same features. It's available in four

-styles. The Omega Lites are smaller, 8^1/$_2$-inch bags that are obviously lighter but have many of the same features in a long, lean, sleek design that comes in seven styles.

The Hampton II Series. A stylish series of bags with a pebble-grain leather look and cross-woven fabric, the Hamptons are freestanding carry/cart bags that come in five styles.

Also from Mizuno are the T-Zoid and Tour Series with the Mizuno name proudly displayed, the Sierra Series, the Metropolitan Series, and the Ultra Stand and Zunos Stand lines that both have a dual-strap system for less strain on your shoulder and an easy-open stand.

Taylor Made

Taylor Made has seen an 80 percent growth rate in bag sales over the past couple of years thanks to new features and better marketing. Bags are specially designed and have a large international market.

Pacesetters. The Pacesetter line features the Grand-stand, the lighter Walk-A-Bout, and the top-of-the-line Deluxe. All of these have easy-open stand mechanisms so you don't have to bend for your bag. There are several pockets for balls and rain gear and a comfortable strap designed for lugging the bag for the full 18 holes or more. Bags range from 8 to 10^1/$_2$ inches in diameter. Taylor Made also offers travel covers for the Pacesetter series. These covers are carefully constructed with foam padding to with-stand the rigors of airline travel.

The Cart Bag. A cart bag (as the name would imply), this 9-inch model includes three jumbo pockets, two smaller pockets, and two full-length garment pockets so you can press a suit while playing. All pockets face outward for easy access. A rain or travel hood is included as is a four-way padded top for club protection. The Cart Bag also has a separate slot for the putter on the outside to give you easy access.

The Home Pro Bag. A durable cart bag, the Home Pro includes five zippered pockets, two mesh pockets, and one Velcro pocket. A 9-inch bag with four full-length dividers, this stylish, well-built model has easily accessible ball pockets and a built-in hood.

Taylor Made also makes other models including the Tour Staff.

Wilson

Wilson has been in the bag business for over 75 years. The company is among the biggest worldwide in golf merchandise with a greater emphasis on a narrower focused product line. In other words, less choices than years ago, but featuring the right options and features that consumers want.

Mountain Pak and Mountain Pak Light. Mountain Pak bags are 8 inches in diameter and feature a six-way club divider and eight pockets including a large side pocket. A long polyester or nylon bag with leather trim, the various models come in a range of colors with an insulated beverage pocket (bottle included), a rain cover, and a choice of single or double straps. Mountain Paks come with or without a stand. The Mountain Pak Jr. series is slightly smaller for the junior golfer and offers many of the same features.

Carry Light Extreme. This lightweight, basic bag from Wilson comes in three styles, giving you a choice of color and either nylon or polyester. The Carry Lites are 8-inch bags with three-way club dividers. Carry Lights also come with a ball pocket and a spacious clothing pocket.

SP3X. Unlike C3P0 and R2D2, the SP3X is not a Star Wars character. It's a series of lightweight nylon or polyester golf bags. The carry-bag series includes a six-way club divider, four pockets, and an optional stand.

Country Club Valet. A top-of-the-line cart bag at either 9 or 10 inches, the Valet has six-way club dividers with graphite protection, 12 pockets of all sizes, a rain hood, and a convenient key clip and wallet pouch. There's also a Ladies Valet, which is designed to do everything but hand you your clubs.

Wilson also makes carryalls and club cases to accompany most of their models. Other models include the bright red Staff Series with the giant Wilson logo, the stylish Country Club Classic, the Prestige II, Clubhouse bags styled after the Valet series, and the Trail Pak and Trail Pak Expedition lines, which follow closely in the footsteps of the Mountain Pak series. Wilson also makes NFL logos for your bag so that, even if you're out on the course on a Sunday, you still can root for your favorite team.

Others

Other golf-bag makers include Bullet, Daiwa, Gemini, Izzo (who created the famous dual strap), Maxfli, Miller, Ping, Sun Mountain (who developed the X-strap system with wrap-around spine pocket for easy access while walking), and Top Flite.

Chapter 4

Golf Shoes

Stepping onto the golf course means stepping into a pair of golf shoes. As with all other components of the game, a wide variety of golf shoes are available. Leading manufacturers including Footjoy, Etonic (from the folks at Spalding), Nike, and Reebok all offer a variety of styles at a wide range of prices—from $40 shoes to $500 top-of-the-line pairs.

The first things you should be looking for in a golf shoe are comfort and fit followed by waterproofing, durability, and fashion. You'll also be looking at softer, metal alternatives to traditional spikes because they are in vogue these days. All these considerations, however, have to fall into your price range. Like all aspects of the game, you'll determine how much you want to spend by how devoted you are to the game. Therefore, you'll probably be asking yourself a question such as, "What is the best shoe I can buy for somewhere between $80 and $130?"

Golf shoes, like any other shoes, are made from different materials, generally variations of leather. A better quality of leather might provide a longer-lasting, more comfortable shoe, but it also will cost you more. A less expensive pair of shoes might be perfect for a golfer who only plays a few times a year because the shoes will not get much wear and tear. Nonetheless, they must be comfortable, and you'll definitely want waterproofing.

Waterproofing

When you buy running shoes, waterproofing generally is not a consideration unless you jog the streets of Venice. When playing golf, however, you'll encounter casual water in the form of puddles on the course and recently sprinkled or watered fairways and greens. You also might land just close enough but not actually in a water hazard. If you set up early-morning tee times, you'll surely find a significant amount of morning dew. Therefore, stepping in water usually is par for the course (pun intended).

Golf shoes are waterproofed in several manners. Some have closed-up tighter seams; others go through a more complicated tanning process. Many affordable yet high-quality shoes have specially designed materials such as *Gore-Tex* between the lining and the outer leather (or other material). Without getting into the technical aspects, you need some form of waterproofing in your golf shoes. The better the waterproofing, the longer the guarantee you'll receive from the manufacturer. An avid player should look for at least a one-year, if not a two-year, waterproofing guarantee. It's also important to look for a shoe with a waterproofing system that breathes. This means it won't allow water drops in but it will allow water vapor out so your feet won't sweat and you'll be more comfortable.

The Spike Issue

Traditional metal spikes gave way to new softer spikes in the 1990s, partly because of new technology and partly because of new course guidelines. Many courses now have "soft spike only" policies. In fact, nearly 5,000 courses in the United States have banned metal spikes as of late 1998. The new policy came about out of concern for the environment and in an effort to lighten the load of golf course superintendents. Metal spikes take a greater toll on the grasses that make up a course. Consequently, there's more wear on the course and a greater degree of maintenance is required, particularly on the greens.

Many golfers also find that, because of soft spikes, they get a truer roll on the green without cleat marks interfering. Soft-spike shoes also can be more comfortable to wear. Most soft spikes are made from a hard plastic that's both durable and not slippery on hard surfaces, such as en route to the locker room. Ceramic spikes also are available. They are very durable but are more expensive.

The reason for wearing spikes is to grip the turf. The durability of cleats is based on the material from which the cleat is made and how often you walk in your cleats on hard surfaces. If you change your shoes shortly after leaving the course (as opposed to wearing them in the locker room, the parking lot, while driving home, and so on), a good set of cleats can last you 50 rounds of golf. Various companies make claims about how long their cleats should last. Some are dual color so you'll know when to change the spikes as the "lower" color will start to appear.

Most modern golf shoes also enable you to change cleats without having to buy a new shoe. If you look for a shoe with 7 or 8 cleats as opposed to the traditional 12 and for cleats that are easy to change, you'll be saving yourself some trouble when the cleats wear down. Many companies now use a new *key lock system* (or something similar). This quick-changing cleat fits in with just a quarter turn as opposed to more traditional cleats, which took a number of turns to get into the shoe.

Cleats, also called spikes, can run from $7 to $20 depending on the material and how easily they can be replaced.

The biggest concern with all the new alternative and soft spikes is whether they'll grip the turf, as well as the old metal ones. Overall, golfers now wearing alternative spikes seem pleased with the traction from the latest models that have been rigorously tested. After all, if something is going to actually make it onto the courses and be endorsed by the leading golf companies, you'd better believe it has been through a lot of testing.

A combination of soft spikes and traction points built into the shoes is the latest technology from a host of companies now battling tooth and nail to create the ideal golf shoe for the future. Because the courses are saying *no more metal cleats*, golf shoe makers know that even long-time golfers will be hanging up their old golf shoes for the new alternative-spike shoes.

And Finally ...

A couple of other things to keep in mind when buying shoes are style and weight. Style is a personal preference. Numerous variations of the old saddle shoes are still on courses around the world. The variety of looks and choices of leather are not unlike shopping for any other type of shoes. If you really want to impress people, you can always buy Genuin's Rio Women's golf shoes made of crocodile—retailing for nearly $800.

As for weight, with all the different components—leather outers, Gore-Tex or another waterproofing system, spikes, and so on—you might simply find that the shoe becomes too heavy. Most manufacturers are aware of this and try to keep their shoes rather lightweight. Nonetheless, it's one more comparison you might take into consideration when deciding between two shoes. If it feels heavy in the store, it's going to feel that much heavier walking up a steep hill on the 16th hole while pulling your cart. Don't go crazy over this area but keep it in the back of your mind.

As for taking care of your shoes, see the section "Take Good Care of Your Golf Shoes" at the end of this chapter.

Dexter

This Massachusetts shoe maker features traditional shoes built to keep water out. Three-year waterproof guarantees highlight the Liberty line, the latest from this well-respected, successful player in the crowded golf-shoe market. Various styles of shoes are offered for everyone from the junior to the senior player with removable footbeds, all moderately priced.

Dexter's Liberty collection. Featuring 10 styles of shoes with three-year waterproof guarantees, the Liberty line includes removable footbeds, reactive soft spikes, and a dual-density outsole for a $100 retail price. The Liberty collection also features 209 traction points per pair, or 145 per foot, if you're counting on much improved footing on any surface.

Dexter's Metropolis. The "Metro" is a new light-weight shoe with a two-year waterproof guarantee. It also has a removable footbed.

Dunlop

Dunlop also offers its own line of lightweight, breathable, waterproof golf shoes. The models are traditional yet styl-ish saddle shoes and are reasonably priced.

Dunlop M7900. This premiere two-year spikeless shoe features a breathable waterproof membrane and combines comfort, tremendous support, and durability. The shoes are carefully designed with 174 points of contact, eight-sided treads, and dual-density wearbars to give you traction on all surface conditions. In short, these shoes should hug the road or, in this case, the course.

Dunlop M5150. Okay, so the names aren't too catchy. The shoe, however, is an inexpensive saddle shoe with a six-month waterproof guarantee and a

lining designed to minimize foot perspiration. A
triple layer in the sole and outsoles are built to
maximize balance and lateral support.

Dunlop W4600CS. This is a comfortable spikeless
woman's shoe for the course, the car, a picnic, or
whatever. A triple-layer insole and soft genuine
leather make this a quality shoe at a good price with
a six-month waterproof guarantee.

Etonic

Etonic was among the leaders in the move from metal
spikes to alternative (softer) spikes. A major competitor in
the golf shoe game, Etonic offers eight or nine types of
shoes with different styles and colors giving you nearly
100 variations from which to choose. Nearly 150 players
on the pro tours wear Etonic shoes. They also are using
the new Q-Lok spike system on most of their shoes so
they don't waste time screwing in spikes.

Etonic Stabilite Turfgrips. Offered in a dozen men's
and women's styles, this shoe is made from
presoftened leather for comfort with waterproof
leather to keep out the elements. New, easy-to-
change, green-friendly, turfgrip, nonmetal cleats
give you traction and stability. The Stabilite is very
popular and is priced under $100.

Etonic All Performance. As Ed Sullivan would have
said, this is "a really good shoe." The All Performance is priced just over $100 and is designed as a
shoe that will last. In fact, it comes with a two-year
durability guarantee. The Etonic All Performance has
a soft-spike sole design so you can wear it anywhere
(well, maybe not to dinner parties). The Gore-Tex
lining keeps water out and is guaranteed for two
years.

Etonic Difference Tour. Offered in both men's and
women's styles, this new shoe has full-leather

everything for comfort. Turfgrip, nonmetal cleats should give you traction and stability, and they are very easy to replace. The Gore-Tex lining sports a two-year waterproof guarantee. The Difference Tour can be had for $150 to $185.

Etonic Ultimate 2000. The cream of the Etonic crop, the Ultimate has presoftened, breathable, French calfskin leather uppers, a leather lining, and a cushioned leather footbed. The shoes are designed to make you so comfortable that you might forget your game and focus exclusively on your feet. A Q-lock quick-release system makes it easy to change the nonmetal Turf Grip cleats. Gore-Tex waterproofing rounds out this men's-only shoe priced near $300.

Footjoy

As the leader of the golf-shoe industry for more than 50 years, Footjoy offers a large assortment of men's and women's shoes ranging from $50 to $250 in retail price plus several models of shoes for juniors. By the summer of 1999, all models should sport the Fast Twist cleat-insertion system. Dryjoys and Softjoys are among the leading lines. In recent years, Footjoy has joined the movement toward steel-spike alternatives by providing soft-spike cleats designed to be lightweight, comfortable, and more green friendly.

Footjoy's Dryjoys GX. The top-of-the-line combination model, this new addition to the Footjoy lineup combines a membrane-leather waterproof system with a two-year guarantee. The new Uni-Tech outsole is designed for traction and stability. This hi-tech durability is a plus because these shoes are built to last.

Footjoy's Dryjoys. As the name implies, this popular golf shoe has a leather waterproof system to keep you dry and, therefore, joyful. These soft-spike shoes retail for around $150 and are lighter than the GX model.

Footjoy's Dryjoy Turfmasters. Dual-rubber outsoles and a custom-fit arch within make these very comfortable soft-spike shoes. IntelliShield membranes are Footjoy's latest way of saying that these shoes will keep you dry, and they guarantee them for two years.

Footjoy's Softjoy Terrains. These lighter, less expensive, soft-spike shoes are carefully designed for comfort. They also come with a one-year water-proofing guarantee.

Mizuno

Among the golf shoe leaders, Mizuno emphasizes comfort and backs it up with a 30-day comfort guarantee. How you prove discomfort is your problem. Nonetheless, Mizuno shoes feature stability and side-to-side flexibility. The new T-Zoid Waves and a variety of Zunos highlight the line, most of which retail for a little over $100.

Mizuno's T-Zoid Waves. Perhaps the coolest name in golf shoes, the T-Zoid Waves are carefully designed for stability and comfort. Five, that's right, five layers provide flexibility and breathability while daring water to get in. Specially designed plates in the forefoot and the heel give you added cushioning. Slightly longer Advantrax spikes help you with traction.

Mizuno's Zunos Series. The Zunos all feature Tread Lite soft spikes, come with two-year waterproofing guarantees, and are designed for comfort. The Bucs, Trailblazers, Mudrakers, and Walkers are all variations of the same theme with different styles for your choice of look.

Mizuno's MIZ Milan. A waterproof full-grain leather upper that is both soft and breathable highlights this latest women's shoe from Mizuno. The shoes come with Mizuno's Tred Lite spikes, which give you good traction with a green-friendly feel.

Nike

The leader in athletic footwear, Nike became a major player in the golf shoe world in the 1990s. Part of Nike's rise is due to the high visibility of tour stars such as Tiger Woods, Hal Sutton, and Ben Crenshaw wearing Nikes on the course during tournaments.

Although the success of the NikeTour has nothing to do with your shoe-shopping needs, it does indicate that Nike is serious about golf. This is worth mentioning because the tour is a training ground for PGA players and is a huge contributor to charity.

Billing their new innovations as *T&C Technology* (traction and contact technology), Nike is trying to provide shoes that are green-friendly while still helping you anchor your feet for better shot-making. The biggest problem when buying shoes from Nike is differentiating between the various Air models. They offer Air Zooms, Air Access, Air Visi, Air Max, Air Stick, and Air Launch. Perhaps a shoe for warm weather is on the horizon—Air Conditioner. Nike golf shoes range from around $50 to the rare Air Limitados at $500 retail.

Nike's Air Zoom Tour T&C. Contact points for traction, three layers of Gore Tex to keep water away, and the new Q-Lok rapid spike-replacement system highlight this shoe, which is carefully crafted to take the golf swing into account.

Nike's Air Max Drive T&C. Complete with the famous Nike Air-Sole heel, this new men's shoe is athletically styled with traction and contact technology to fit players of all levels. A comfortable shoe with waterproof leather, the Air Max is reasonably priced at under $100.

Nike's Air Launch T&C. A good basic men's shoe for newer players, the Air Launch model won't launch your drives into orbit, but it will keep your feet dry, help you maintain traction, and give you a comfortable feel for around $75.

Nike's Air Draw T&C. A leather, lightweight, waterproof woman's golf shoe, the Air Draw is designed to give golfers of all levels an athletic fit, comfort, and traction on the course for around $100. This shoe also has the heel air-sole unit and easy-to-change spikes.

Nike's Air Visi TW T&C. Featuring *Nike's Moisture Management System*—full-grain leather with Gore-Tex to keep water out—this is billed as Tiger's game-day shoe. Traction and comfort technology, easy-to-change waffle spikes, and excellent stability highlight this model, which retails for $160.

Nike's Air Zoom Tenaci's. An Italian-made, Algonquin-style shoe that features a calfskin-leather upper and leather outsoles, this top-of-the-line shoe is designed for comfort, stability, and traction. T&C traction at contact and the famed air in the heels also are part of this $300 pair of shoes.

Reebok

A major player in the world of athletic shoes, Reebok features several models of men's and women's soft-spike shoes including the Convertibles, the DNX line, and Monterey's. Reebok's shoes are relatively lightweight, are moderately priced, and feature the popular Quick-Loc spike-replacement system.

Reebok Convertible and Convertible CST. These are leather-lined, comfortable, rubber shoes. The top-of-the-line models feature the *Aqua-Shield waterproof membrane*, which is the Reebok answer to H2O. The shoes retail for under $120.

Reebok DMX Trac. This is one of the premier new spikeless shoes designed to provide extra traction while being extremely comfortable. The shoes feature a raised tread pattern that hugs the ground when you swing and that provides stability when you walk—including up and down golf course hills. There are also 23 (tiny) interconnected chambers to move air from the heel to the front of the shoe. Basically, there's a lot going on in this reasonably priced, popular shoe.

Others

Another player in the golf shoe business is Florsheim. A major manufacturer in the real world of men's shoes for more than 100 years, Florsheim sent its technical staff out to find something new and innovative. They came back with the first MagneForce golf shoe. The idea is to increase blood flow to the feet and thus provide more energy to the legs by inserting tiny magnets in the insoles of the shoes. In addition to the *holistic benefits* of having magnets in your shoes, you also should find all the loose change on the course. The biomagnetic shoes have a 30-day comfort guarantee, come with the popular Q-Lok easy-to-change spikes, and are offered in a variety of styles.

The folks at Rockport are convinced that the spike wars will lead to no need for spikes at all. They are offering an affordable line of spikeless golf shoes carefully molded for traction. In an effort to show that you need not bother with replaceable spikes, Rockport also offers a resoling program for the life of the shoe.

For ladies who like the comfort of sandals, you also can find golf sandals. Spiked or spikeless, open-toe sandals can be bought from Sandbaggers Enterprises, Inc., in Lewiston Maine (800-659-9607). No, they won't keep water out, but they are hand-crafted from fine leather and are designed to be very comfortable—particularly on a hot day.

Other golf-shoe makers include: Adidas, Ashworth, Back Bay, Bite, Eastland, EZ Step, Hi-Tech Golf, Greg Norman, Johnston & Murphy, Lady Fairway, New Balance, Niblick, Tags, Wilson, and Walter Genuin.

Take Good Care of Your Golf Shoes

If you take care of golf shoes, obviously they'll last longer. Using a shoe tree or keeping rolled-up paper (if you're lazy) inside the shoes helps them retain their shape. Cleaning off the cleats helps them help you by allowing them to hug the turf. Wiping off the outer portion of each shoe keeps the shoes breathable. Because they are waterproof, you should be able to wash them off. Hosing shoes down, however, can hurt the shape.

If you can afford two pairs of golf shoes, you obviously will have shoes around that much longer. Like many golfers, you'll probably use one pair for better course conditions and the other pair for the day after a downpour when you'll be tracking through mud and muck. Whether you have one pair or two, it's to your advantage to buy replacement spikes and to check periodically to see if your spikes are worn down.

Chapter 5

Golf Gloves

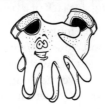

Golf gloves were created years ago to help players deal with cooler conditions. If you've ever experienced the sting on your hands from your club meeting the ball, you'll immediately understand the need for a glove.

Over the years, manufacturers have carefully researched and improved the golf glove. They've added numerous features to prevent the hand from perspiring and to keep water out. The modern golf glove is designed to keep your hand dry and is made to fit comfortably. *Cabretta* leather is the fabric of choice for flexibility and durability. It is a softer leather than that which is used on jackets and leather accessories. The glove also needs to be thin to give you maximum feel.

Although some golfers never bother with a glove at all, it's simply part of the game for most. For golfers with small hands or hands prone to perspiration, a glove can prove particularly helpful. A good glove should be tight enough that it does not move around while it's on your hand; however, it should not be so tight as to restrict movement or be uncomfortable. The best glove is one that is breathable so your hand will not become sweaty. This also is important for a golfer who takes the glove off for extra feel when putting. Sweaty palms don't get that desired feel when gripping your putter.

Golfers generally use one glove: Righties buy a glove for the left hand and visa versa. The idea is that the opposite hand is gripping the club with the palm and fingers tightly wrapped around it. The other hand is guiding, steering, or controlling, for lack of a better term.

When buying golf gloves, look for your size. Make sure the glove goes up to and closes snugly around your wrist. Most modern-day gloves close with Velcro or a snap. The bottom line is that the glove should fit comfortably so you can essentially forget it's there and can focus on the task of hitting the ball.

As with everything else, technology has created new and improved golf gloves, some of which are designed to allow the proper flexibility at various points in your swing. Although such features are well intended, the bottom line is that you should find a glove that fits comfortably, is breathable, and is durable. Some well-thought-out features on women's gloves include enough room for engagement rings (or their stones) and cut-out fingertips for manicured nails. Beyond these little (although sometimes useful) gimmicks, men's and women's gloves generally differ only in sizes.

A single golf glove should run you anywhere from $5 to $20, depending on whether it's made from Cabretta leather, a synthetic material, or a mixture of the two. Leather gloves will feel better and will last longer, but they might cost more and not give you quite the same *feel* on the club as the synthetic/leather combinations. Manufacturers are making leather gloves that are water resistant, breathable, and designed to enhance feel. Again, it's a matter of choice and comfort.

Several companies sell sets of three gloves for $25 to $40. Gloves usually are white, although black and other colors do exist. They come in the basic sizes: small, medium, large, extra large, and extra-extra large. It's a good idea to have three or four gloves because even the best won't last forever, particularly if you play often and react to a bad shot by ripping off the glove and tossing it.

The following sections discuss some of the golf gloves from which you can choose. See the section "Take Care of Your Gloves" for information on making your glove last.

Daiwa

The Team Daiwa line of gloves includes the Ulti Mitt, Soft Mitt, Pro Mitt, and All Weather Pro Mitt. The Ulti and Soft models are made of sheepskin and Cabretta. They are designed to be comfortable and durable. Daiwa gloves also are made with a special palm fit that keeps the palm taut. They are Scotchgarded, and the fingers are ventilated for breathability so your hand will not sweat. You also can have your glove custom embroidered to impress whomever you meet and shake hands with on the course.

Dunlop

The Advanced Performance Gloves from Dunlop feature a select, premium Cabretta leather palm for superior feel with a micro fiber back to enhance fit. The micro fiber technology is Dunlop's way of giving you very breathable yet durable gloves. These gloves are designed to enhance your performance in all playing conditions. In other words, they should keep your hands warm, dry, and sweat-free for the entire round.

Etonic

From the folks at the shoe and glove division of Spalding comes the Etonic Difference. The Difference has a 100 percent full Cabretta leather palm and fingers. Cool Max inserts at flex points allow the glove to be breathable in the fingers to prevent sweating. The stylish glove has a synthetic back and is carefully designed for enhanced comfort.

Footjoy

The golf shoe kings say why make shoes without matching gloves? The Sta-Sof model is designed to be extremely comfortable, and it's tanned for water resistance. The Sta-Sof Alliance is Cabretta leather with a synthetic back, giving you a comfortable, slightly thinner glove. The Sof Joy is 100 percent Cabretta leather and is designed for comfort. The Weather-Sof and Junior Weather Sof also are part of the Sof line. There's also a winter line for those die-hards who want to play in the northeast in December. The fancier Footjoy Spider is a graphite-enhanced, textured-leather glove with an elastic back.

Ben Hogan

Ben didn't wear gloves, but after enough calluses, he (and his designers) realized the need for them. The Hogan Apex gloves feature Australian Reserve Leather, which is 10 to 15 percent thinner than Cabretta leather. The idea is to give the golfer a gloveless feel. The Apex gloves also have fiber between the fingers to maintain a consistent fit, and they are breathable and durable. Hogan also makes two soft Leader gloves, which also include the between-finger fiber and are quite durable.

Mizuno

Someone had to do it, so why not the techno gang at Mizuno? One of the premiere worldwide sporting goods manufacturers, Mizuno has taken the hottest material in modern day golf—titanium—and is using it to tan their new line of golf gloves, the Ti-Flex. The Cabretta leather gloves are tanned with titanium particles to produce a glove that's ultra soft and is more durable than much of the competition. The new, popular Ti-Flex gloves also are water and perspiration resistant as well as machine washable. Also in the Mizuno line of gloves are the Techno Flex, Grip Flex, and Miz gloves.

Precept

If Nick Price and Raymond Floyd can wear these gloves, so
can you. If only you could hit as well as they! Precept's
Tour Glove is a water-resistant, Cabretta leather glove
with dual-finger ventilation for both breathability and
comfort. The Precept Grip Glove and Lady Grip Glove
combine Cabretta leather with synthetics and are designed for comfort, water resistance, and durability. Both
offer a palm patch that enhances the life of the glove.

Titleist

The Titleist Players Glove also is made from Cabretta
leather. These gloves are breathable and therefore are perspiration resistant as well as comfortable. They also are designed to ensure maximum club feel. The Perma Soft
Glove is a soft, smooth glove that is designed to fit well
while resisting moisture. The Perma Grip Glove adds digital leather to the thumb and palm for added flexibility
and an improved grip. Titleist gloves can be custom
crested with your choice of emblem, and there are a number of custom packages. They also are tested for thinness
and *feel*.

Wilson

The Wilson Ultra series includes the Tour, Select, Grip,
Flex, and Junior models. The top-of-the-line Tour model
features special Lycra inserts to enhance breathability and
fit. Both the Tour and Select models benefit from a special
tanning process to keep external moisture and perspiration out. The Grip model, as the name might indicate,
offers a more sophisticated palm design for a better grip
on the club. All models except the Flex are made from
Cabretta leather. All models of the popular Wilson line
have breathable fingers, sport the Wilson W logo, and are
durable.

Others

Other leading glove makers include Tommy Armour, Maxfli, Nike, Powerbilt, Reebok, and Slazenger.

If you want a glove that doubles as a scorekeeper, a company in New Jersey called Scoremaster is making a line of men's and women's soft, Cabretta leather gloves called the Par Score Glove. The glove has a digital scorer sewn into the back that keeps track of par, the number of strokes per hole, and the number of strokes per round. But do you really want to know how you're doing every time you look at your grip on the club?

Take Care of Your Gloves

Gloves often are made of durable leather so they will last. A glove should not start to tear after a couple rounds. Nonetheless, it helps if you take care of the glove. To help ensure that your golf glove lasts, you should do the following:

- Put the glove on by putting your fingers in first and easily sliding the glove up your hand. If you get into the habit of simply pulling it on from the end, it is more likely to tear sooner.

- Wipe dirt off the glove before putting it away and straighten the glove out.

- Don't keep a golf glove in a particularly warm place because too much heat or sunlight will dry out the leather. In fact, it might be best to keep the glove in the original packaging or in a similar plastic bag.

- Lay a wet golf glove out and let it dry before putting it away.

You don't need to spend a lot of time taking care of your golf gloves, but it doesn't hurt to get into good habits so they'll last longer.

Chapter 6

Golf Clothing

Loose, comfortable clothes in sporty styles typify the latest in fashions for the golf course. Wind- and rain-resistant outerwear also is carefully engineered to keep the elements from infringing on your game.

Major clothing designers such as Tommy Hilfiger, Giorgio Armani, and Ralph Lauren all have lines of sporty attire. Many golf equipment and accessories manufacturers also provide fashionable clothing—often at better prices and designed more closely with the movements of the game in mind.

Looking fashionable on the course can boost your confidence and enhance your game, and having the right weather-resistant clothing ready in your bag will help you get through the full 18 holes.

When buying clothes for the course, you want to look for the following.

- **Comfort.** Nonrestricting and nonbinding clothes allow you to swing freely.

- **Pockets.** From tees to ball markers, you'll always need pockets on the golf course. Velcro or zipper pockets can keep items from falling out when you're bending to tee up or pulling your ball from the cup.

- **Colors.** Light colors reflect the sun; darker colors absorb it. Choose accordingly. If you're prone to perspiration, you might want a lighter color on a sunny day.

- **Fabrics that breathe.** Clothes that keep wind and rain out but that won't make you sweat are advantageous.

Sport shirts and long pants—or skirts (or shorts) and lightweight tops for women—usually are the uniform of the game. Some clubs have dress codes, however, which usually say no halters, cutoffs, T-shirts or shorts. Some courses will insist on a collared shirt. Beyond that, you're on your own.

Inclement Weather

Most people don't usually make a habit of setting out to play in the pouring rain. Anyone who plays weekly, however, will attest to the fact that they've been rained on from time to time. Rain gear, therefore, is part of the golfer's arsenal. The two most important words to know when it comes to rain gear are Gore-Tex. A specially developed rainproof, windproof, yet breathable material, Gore-Tex (from W.L. Gore and Associates) is a unique, patented invention used in the best-quality outerwear.

Major manufacturers including Etonic, Forrester, MacGregor, Nike, Sun Ice, and Zero Restriction all utilize Gore-Tex. This material contains numerous tiny pores that do not let water in but that allow the material to breathe. If Gore-Tex is too expensive for you, however, other materials are available. Look for a waterproof guarantee and some degree of breathability so you won't perspire.

Many rain outfits include hoods, but you also might want a water-resistant hat. Your hat, as well as your rain gear, should fit nicely into your bag. Caps are good for guarding against the sun, but they might not do the trick on seaside links. Many companies—including some of the ones covered in the following sections—make caps because it's good for advertising and marketing. When wearing a cap or hat on the course, make sure it fits snugly (adjustable ones are great) because the last thing you need is a hat flying off whenever you swing.

The following sections discuss a few golf manufacturers and selections from their clothing lines.

Cleveland

The Staff Windshirt from Cleveland is a breathable, micropolyester pullover for men, that is both wind resistant and water repellent. Also available is the Staff Sweatshirt made from heavyweight material and the new water- and wind-resistant (Ultratex) Performance Windshirt with a half-zip fleece collar.

Cleveland also offers long-sleeve, 100 percent cotton Oxford shirts; heavy duty T-shirts; and lightweight, loose-fitting golf shirts. Wool, six-panel *Wedge*, *Relaxed Fit*, and *Tour Authentic* caps are among the Cleveland headgear.

Cross Creek

Cross Creek shirts are a staple on any golf course. They are comfortable, sporty, yet sophisticated shirts designed to let you feel good and look good on the course and in the clubhouse. The latest line includes ladies' apparel and a couple of items for the younger set as well as the tradi-

tion includes

lannel style created by a mélange of hades.

- **Woodlands.** Features gray flannel combined with lush textures.

- **Core Solids and Pacific Time.** Features fashionable stripes and geometric designs in bright colors and crisp white.

Descente

Among the fashions from Descente are Jacquard and Herringbone Polo shirts, which are 100 percent cotton and are designed to be comfortable while playing and walking the course. Lightweight yet warm fleece vests and a water-repellent, micro fiber corduroy jacket with front and rear ventilation and two flap-over-button pockets also are part of the Descente ensemble. For added protection against the sun, Descente's new Sport Collection shirts are made from a new fabric that the company says will block 90 percent of UV rays, which can absorb through thin shirts.

Forrester

Forrester has specialized in manufacturing performance golf wear since 1983. The latest line of first-rate, high-quality micro fiber Gore-Tex jackets, pants, and hats (for both men and women) are designed to keep you dry while being comfortable on the course. All are windproof, lightweight, breathable, and of course, waterproof. Both long and short jackets are offered. Full water-resistant, Gore-Tex–lined rainsuits with well-placed pockets, back vents, and matching hats also are available.

A Polar Tec fleece line also is popular from Forrester. It includes vests; lightweight, quiet, nylon, reversible pullovers; and jackets. The ultra-light line is warm, soft, flexible, and comfortable.

MacGregor

MacGregor is the company behind Tourney out one of the premier names in golf apparel. The pullovers and jackets for men are waterproof, windproof, and fully seam sealed. Pullovers come with high Anorak collars, adjustable-snap wrist cuffs, and are designed to be comfortable as well as durable. There's also a soft, low-collar pullover for year-round wear with a rib-knit collar, cuffs, and a waistband.

Several jackets from Tourney feature what are called *radial player sleeves*, which are engineered to not inhibit motion. Two lined, reverse pockets and an inside scorecard pocket with Velcro should hold all your on-course odds and ends. Other jackets are available as well as pants with 12-inch leg zippers and wind flaps, plenty of pockets, and cinch snaps at the ankles. A variety of bucket hats also are available to keep your head dry so you can use it to plan your next shot.

The Tourney women's line includes a series of short and midlength jackets. These feature side snaps for easy access to pants pockets and draw strings for an adjustable fit. Women's pants and bucket hats also are available.

Mizuno

Mizuno offers a line of performance rainwear including a full-zip jacket, a half-zip jacket, a vest, and pants. A three-layer structure is designed for enhanced comfort. The fabric is specially treated to be durable, water repellent, and breathable. The collection is windproof, and the seam-sealed construction keeps moisture out. The Performance Collection is designed to complement the motions of the golfer on the course. Adjustable leg openings and storm flaps also are featured.

The *Silenzz* Zip Neck Windshirt and Crew Neck Windshirt are both micro fiber designed with what Mizuno calls "the ultimate noise control system." The zip neck has a nine-inch zipper and two side-seam pockets and is made to be durable, breathable, stain resistant, windproof, and water resistant. The crew neck has a lower neck with a tight micro weave, two side-seam pockets, and a soft nylon liner for those less-brutal days on the links.

The Marathon Nylon Crew Neck Windshirt is a lightweight shirt that also provides rain and wind resistance and is soft and quiet in its construction. The Cotton Interlock Mock Turtleneck is a 100 percent yarn-dyed cotton shirt for comfort on cooler days. It has a straight-hemmed bottom and strong cover-stitched seams to strengthen armholes and shoulders. All Mizuno shirts come in Medium through XX-Large and in a choice of colors.

Greg Norman

From Greg Norman comes a line of men's shirts crafted to be comfortable and stylish. Along with long-sleeve, mock turtlenecks made from Egyptian cotton are wind shirts made of 100 percent nylon. These are wind and water resistant and very comfortable. Polo shirts featuring stylish modern patterns are made from lightweight cotton and feature the famous Greg Norman shark logo.

The color-blocked sweater is a smart cotton garment with knit cuffs and a waistband. There is a wide range of styles in shirts and sweaters plus Italian belts offered by the folks at Norman. There's also a new line of casual dress and athletic golf hosiery (socks) designed, manufactured, and marketed by American Essentials.

Reebok

The shoe kings at Reebok also make quality apparel for the golf course. In addition to a variety of soft Polo shirts, Reebok also makes a windproof vest that keeps you warm while freeing up your arms for flexibility. The vest has a banded waist to stay snug while swinging and is water resistant and lined. The Packable Jacket is designed to be just that—easy to cram into the bag when the temperature goes up between the front and back nines. The jacket is 100 percent nylon, is water resistant, and has pockets and cuffs with Velcro to keep them closed.

Sun Mountain

This Montana-based company offers a mountain of clothes to cover you on the course in all weather conditions. Highlighting the rain gear are the Tempest pants with an extra breathable layer of protection from the elements plus roomy zippered pockets and access to your pants pockets underneath. The lower legs zip open so they can slide easily over your shoes.

The Cumulous and Sigmet rain jackets are made from high-quality micro fiber and are waterproof. The sleeve cuffs on the Sigmet model use both Velcro and elastic to keep water out. The Cirrus rain suit (both jacket and pants) is constructed of coated micro fibers with a drawstring waist, zippered lower-leg pockets, and zippered adjustable vents. The Altos, also a pants and jacket set, includes a taffeta lining in a well-conceived, weather-resistant outfit.

For golfers who don't know when to call it a day, Sun Mountain offers the Typhoon Reversible, which features a coated micro fiber seam-sealed solid on one side and plaid or houndstooth on the other. The pullover features a half-zipper collar and zip pockets in a durable, comfortable garment. Also featured are the Monsoon and Dew Point pullovers and a Stormtight vest.

Wind gear includes the Micro fiber Check, Micro fiber Glen Plaid, and Headwind Micro fiber wind shirts plus Reversible Micro fiber, Westwind, and Micro fiber Solo vests.

Ladieswear includes the Alta Rain Suit with oversized armholes, extended shoulders, and long sleeves designed for free movement. An interior draw cord on the pants allows for adjusted fit. Antique brass hardware on the trim adds a decorative touch. The Typhoon Reversible rain jacket has deep half-pocket construction, contains zipper pockets on seam sides, and is micro fiber and brushed for quiet movement. The ladies Micro fiber line also includes the Check Windjammer, Sierra, Solo Vest, and Headwind. A junior line consists of a couple of jackets and a PGA Tour line featuring the Medalist Rainsuit, Players Jacket, and Tour Rainshirt Reversible.

Taylor Made

Taylor Made makes several affordable, comfortable golf shirts of various styles. The Long Sleeve Mock Turtleneck, Windshirt, and Zipneck Windshirt are designed for cooler days on the links as is the Sueded Mock Tee. Sueded micro fiber makes the shirts durable as well as comfortable. The outerwear pieces are lined with two zip pockets for your smaller course necessities. There's also a traditional sweatshirt that's ideal for on- and off-the-course wear.

The Taylor Made collection (a men's line) is crafted with the golfer in mind. It takes into account the movements associated with the game and the need for comfort and quality. Three styles—the Country Club, Tour, and Fairway collections—offer varying colors and styles of the Taylor Made line.

Zero Restriction

Outerwear from Zero Restriction also features Gore-Tex materials and more. The ZR line of products is very popular with players on the LPGA, PGA, and SPGA Tours as well as with weekend players because it has been carefully designed for comfort without impairing your game.

Zero Restriction jackets expand and retract with the golf swing. This unique expansion and retraction is accomplished with the help of patented telescoping cuffs that allow full freedom at the wrists areas, expansion back pleats, and a stretch liner that works to remove any restriction in the shoulder area. An interior, snug liner-snap system eliminates bulkiness in the front.

Both men's and ladies' styles are available with an emphasis on outerwear that's both wind and rain resistant. In addition to Gore-Tex rain suits, ZR offers Lightweight, Superlight, and Fallweight wind shirts, a collection of Comfortsuede Windstopper pullovers, and a High Grade Series of cashmere jackets, wind shirts, hats, and gloves.

Chapter 7

Odds and Ends

In addition to essentials such as balls, clubs, bags, and the seldom-mentioned tees—which can easily be found at any golf or sporting-goods shop—there are a wealth of other golf-related items. Some are designed to be helpful; others are for decorative purposes and can be quite unnecessary.

The following list contains just a few of the odds and ends you'll find:

> **Character golf balls.** Take a swat at Mickey, Goofy, Donald, or Pluto. The Disney characters are all available on the Pinnacle Character dozen. Other logos, characters, and unique designs also can be found in the novelty section of golf shops with a sense of humor.

> **Club-carrying cases.** Complete with pockets, a padded shoulder strap, plenty of room, plus inner protection for your clubs, this is the only way for your clubs to travel. Some cases even include shoe pockets. SKB makes solid-metal travel cases with locks, hinges, and wheels. Many bags from the retailers in Chapter 3, "Golf Bags," come with matching travel covers.

Club-cleaning kits. This is a nice way to polish your shafts and to keep your clubs clean between rounds. Make sure that, if the kit includes any type of cleaning materials, it is designed for the metal makeup of your particular clubs.

Divot tools. You should have them in your bag. Unfortunately, most players do not replace divots very carefully. It's a good idea to have the equipment, however, so you can do so on occasion.

Electric carts. No, you don't need to go out and buy one. Few people have room for one and even fewer actually own one. Perhaps if you're living in a golf community, they can provide your primary means of travel. Courses that allow electric carts make them readily available. You might want to pick up an electric cart heater for off-season days.

Floppy hats. The famous floppies from Callaway, DryJoy, and other companies are good for blocking the sun.

Golf Monopoly. Yes, it does exist. It's based on the classic game except you buy golf courses.

Hand carts. The vast majority of golfers rent them. In fact, they are part of the green fee at most resort and upscale public courses. They also are available for purchase in some golf retail outlets. Should you want to buy your own, check to make sure it's durable and easy to open and close. Make sure the cart is balanced, has strong wheels, and has a sturdy handle for pulling it around the course. Available brands include Blue Sky Golf, Cart Caddy, Turfmaster, and others. The basic hand cart that slips easily into your trunk with your golf bag will generally run between $60 and $140. A company named Lob Runner makes an electric motorcaddy that you pull, but it uses a 12-volt battery to move along behind you. Built-in cruise control compensates for hills. Unfortunately, it doesn't mow the rough for you. Such remote control carts can run about $500.

Head covers. Not for you, for your clubs! They protect your clubs from the elements and from hitting each other. They come in all styles but certainly are not a necessity. Nike, for example, offers a set of head covers made from dense pile acrylic with knit-sock, stretchable long necks that protect your graphite shafts. Although many covers are knit or acrylic, other companies make them in suede or even fur-lined and with numerous characters to amuse your foursome. Yes, there are even Three Stooges talking head covers!

Indoor putting greens. They can be as long as nine or ten feet, and some even have an automatic ball return. Although they are fun, they don't really help you read real greens unless your home or office is on a hill. Putting tracks or rulers are another possibility. They are long and thin and are supposed to help you align your putts and set them up. They might be more beneficial from a teaching standpoint (but they're not as much fun).

Shag balls. Also known as practice balls, they're the plastic balls, generally with holes in them and are no fun to hit whatsoever. Go to the range and hit something real.

Socks. Footjoy and other companies sell durable, cushioned sole socks to absorb sweat while walking and to keep your feet dry from the elements—although your golf shoes should handle that. You do not need to purchase specific golf socks.

Tees. Don't hit the course without them! A hundred usually can be purchased for around $5 and a thousand will run you $15. There are standard plastic and wooden tees and the primary difference is that plastic ones will last a little longer. There also are tees made with a little plastic back on them to help you hit the ball, but they're illegal! You also can buy personalized tees, which are legal.

Towels. Towels should be small enough to fit in the bag, yet big enough so you can find them deep in the pocket. Callaway, Cobra, Mizuno, Nike, Taylor Made (Burner Bubble Towels), and other major manufacturers offer them. They're good for keeping your hands dry and clean, especially after an encounter with a sandtrap or a search for your ball in the woods or water.

Umbrellas. Golf umbrellas are made by Armour, Callaway, Cobra, Daiwa, Mizuno, Nike, Taylor Made, Wilson, and other equipment manufacturers. They're designed to hook onto your bag. Good golf umbrellas usually exceed 60 inches, open easily, resist wind, and are very durable.

Even the best umbrellas are not sufficient protection against lightning, in fact they can act as a lightning rod. There is no way around it, if you see lightning around where you are playing, simply pack up and call it a day. Lightning has killed golfers and spectators.

Yardage-range finders. They're not allowed in most tournaments, but they're on the market nonetheless. Using a battery, they can help you determine how far away you are from the pin and what club to use. One company advertises a yardage detector that can measure distances up to 800 yards.

It also should be noted that you can find golf wallets, slippers, pens, travel humidors, holiday items and ornaments, cups, clocks, mugs, money clips, key chains, screen savers, desk organizers, barbecue utensils, calendars, watches, tray tables, and even an 18-inch statue of Bugs Bunny leaning on a golf club. Heck, you can even buy a golf scene director's chair! The bottom line is that anything you want can be found with a golf design if you look hard enough.

Major retailers, like those mentioned in the introduction, have some of these items available, while others are found through specialty golf shops all over the country. Also, on the Internet you will find golf merchandisers some of which feature unique items. The best way to find some of these items is to ask other golfers when you see them with certain items, where they purchased them. Golfers love to share information about the great game.

Golf Videos, Books, and Web Sites

There are several different types of golf videos, although the vast majority fall into the educational category. Others offer great moments in the game, golf history, or are simply to entertain. Many instructional videos are made by great players, and videos showing great moments on the tour give you the perfect opportunity to watch how the best players in the world make tough shots look easy. You can learn from watching them closely. The following are a few of the numerous golf videos on the market. They vary in length, style, and subject matter, although the theme (playing better golf) is the same.

The *Golf My Way* tapes provide a great educational series from the one and only Jack Nicklaus. These videos include *Full Swing* and *Hitting The Shots*.

18 Tips from 18 Legends of Golf from Jay Randolph gives you multiple perspectives on the great game of golf.

Dave Leadbetter's tapes provide tips and assistance for golfers at all levels. Videos include *Practice Makes Perfect, From Beginner To Winner, The Full Golf Swing, The Short Game*, and others.

Nice Shot by Chuck—not Ben—Hogan examines the mental side of golf, which is very important.

The *Bobby Jones: How I Play Golf* videos have been popular for a while. They feature *The Long Game, The Short Game*, and *The Complete Game*.

The Dave Stockton Golf Clinic from Dave himself also gives solid lessons for the average golfer.

The Art Of Putting by Ben Crenshaw gives you a 44-minute lesson in getting the ball into the cup.

Dave Peltz's Amazing Truth About Putting also works on the putting game and features Peltz's own methodology.

Golf Shape is a fitness video complete with a 760-page guide book to get you fit for the course.

Beginning Golf for Women by Donna White is a two-tape set that teaches the long and short of the game to ladies.

Ben Sutton's Golf School is available for men and for women.

The *Golf and All It's Glory* series of tapes covers golf's history, tradition, and major tournaments.

For a little entertainment, you also can buy Tim Conway's *Dorf On Golf*, one of Leslie Neilson's *Bad Golf* videos, one of many golf blooper tapes, or the *I Love Lucy* classic golf video. Popular golf movies include *Tin Cup*, *Follow the Sun* (about Ben Hogan), *Happy Gilmore*, and *Caddyshack*.

Most educational golf videos can be found at golf retailers and through their catalogs, at **www.Amazon.com**, or at major video outlets that carry sports and recreational videos. The entertainment videos are, of course, at your local video store.

Golf Books

As with videos, numerous golf books can teach you how to play. There also are books about players, courses, and tournaments such as the Masters. The USGA has a full library at its famous Golf House in Far Hills, New Jersey, stocked from floor to ceiling solely with golf books.

If you're looking to buy books, in addition to Barnes & Noble and Amazon.com, all leading book and golf retailers stock a wide array of golf books. The following are a few examples.

Harvey Penick's *Little Red Book* and *Little Green Book* offer lessons from a legend.

Dave Leadbetter, the premier teacher of the golf swing, has several books on the market including *Golfing Greats*, in which he analyzes the swings of great golfers, *The Golf Swing*, *Positive Practice*, and *Faults and Fixes*.

Golf Is Not A Game of Perfect by Dr. Bob Rotella is one of several books by the mental guru of golf.

Putt Like The Pros by Dave Peltz is the definitive guide to putting.

Golf Magazine's Complete Book Of Golf Instruction by James A. Frank, et al., gives guidance from one of the game's premier periodicals.

Classic Instruction by Bobby Jones tells it like it needs to be told.

Steve Elkington's Five Fundamentals of Golf by Steve Elkington is one of the newer instructional golf books.

The Complete Short Game: The Ultimate Guide To Building and Perfecting Your Chipping, Pitching, Putter and Bunker Play Skills by Ernie Els is another new instructional book with the longest name in the game.

Other great golf books include

Ben Hogan's Five Lessons by Ben Hogan with photos by Herbert Warren Wind

Golf In The Kingdom by Michael Murphy

A Good Walk Spoiled: Days And Nights On The PGA Tour by John Feinstein

Emerald Fairways and Foam Covered Seas: A Golfer's Pilgrimage to the Courses of Ireland by James W. Finegan

The Rules Of Golf by Tom Watson

And Then Arnie Told Chi Chi … More Than 200 of the Best True Golf Stories, Don Wade & Gary McCord

Everything Golf by Rich Mintzer and Peter Grossman

Web Sites

All the major golf manufacturers have Web sites that are easy to find by typing in **www.nameofthecompany** (such as **www.misuno.com**) or by searching for the name at **www.yahoo.com** or another search engine. Other major golf Web sites link you to anything you could possibly want and in some cases to each other. The following are among the largest.

www.igolf has everything from player profiles to equipment, history, and a place to research.

www.golfonline (from *Golf Magazine*) has news, tips, resources, and more.

www.worldgolf.com offers a world of golf information including merchandise and statistics.

www.golfweb.com is another major link that provides courses, books, equipment, and instruction.

www.golfsearch.com puts you in touch with anything you need including 97 retail locations.

www.golfmagazine.com does just that, it links you to *Golf Magazine*, the PGA Tour site, and trivia.

www.pgatour.com gives you a place to follow the pros.

www.planet.eon.net is a Canadian-based site with plenty of links worldwide including the PGA and other tours plus plenty of golf associations.

golf.com offers commentary, classifieds, news, and equipment information.

For equipment and accessories, you might try the following.

www.americancustomgolf links you to a custom club design site.

www.progolf-discount.com is a major golf retailer.

www.edwinwatts.com is another major golf retailer.

www.golfsmith.com is yet another major golf retailer.

www.golf.com (from *Golfday*) also is a major golf retailer.

As previously mentioned, many of these sites serve as a major network and link you to courses, equipment, and numerous other sites. Golf is a very easy subject in which to find what you need on the Web because the sites are so wide-reaching.

Phone List

In case you'd like to receive catalogs on the latest products, get any further information or order products, below are phone numbers for the companies mentioned within the book. (Not included are some companies in the odds and ends section.)

Adams Golf	1-800-622-0609
Adidas	1-888-295-3217
Alien Sport	1-800-989-GOLF
Tommy Armour	1-800-723-4653
Ashworth & Back Bay, and Niblick	1-800-771-9000
Bennington	1-800-624-2580
Bite	1-800-248-3465
Black Ice	1-800-404-9990
Bridgestone (Precept)	1-800-358-6319
Bullet	1-800-842-3781
Burton	1-800-848-7115
Callaway	1-800-228-2767
Carbite	1-800-272-4325
Cleveland	1-800-999-6263
Cobra	1-800-223-3537
Cross Creek	1-800-959-1504
Daiwa	1-800-736-GOLF
Dexter	1-888-833-9837
Douglas	1-800-621-0084
Dunlop—shoes	1-800-331-4938
Dunlop—clubs	1-800-235-5516

Eastland	1-207-865-3149
Edwin Watts	1-800-874-0146
Etonic	1-800-638-6642
EZ Step	1-800-323-1130
Florsheim	1-800-265-7876
Footjoy	1-800-225-8500
Forrester	1-800-556-4653
Gemini	1-813-973-4652
Walter Genuin	1-800-531-2218
Golfsmith	1-800-369-0099
Golf Day	1-800-676-4653
Gregory Paul	1-800-727-0070
Hi Tec	1-800-448-3210
Ben Hogan	1-800-88-Hogan
HPG Ram Tour	1-800-647-8122
Izzo Systems	1-800-284-1220
Johnston & Murphy	1-800-433-7414
Jones Sports	1-800-547-8447
Kunnan	1-800-399-8599
Lady Fairway	1-800-770-5239
LaMode	1-800-678-5246
MacGregor	1-800-841-4358
MaxFli	1-800-768-4727
Miller	1-800-489-2247
Mizuno	1-800-333-7888
New Balance	1-800-622-1218
Nicklaus	1-800-322-1872
Nike	1-800-238-6453
Greg Norman	1-888-667-6264
Odyssey	1-800-487-5664
Orlimar	1-800-917-2288

Ping	1-800-528-0650
Gary Player	1-800-4-Player
Powerbilt	1-800-848-7693
Pro Golf	1-800-Pro-Golf
Ram	1-800-833-4653
Reebok	1-800-454-4005
Slazenger	1-800-766-2615
Sun Mountain	1-800-227-9224
Tags	1-800-585-Tags
Taylor Made	1-800-456-8633
Teardrop	1-800-829-7888
Titleist	1-800-225-8500
Top Flite	1-800-225-6601
Wilson	1-800-622-0444
Wood Brothers	1-800-800-8424
Yonex	1-800-44-Yonex
Zero Restriction	1-800-367-0669
Zevo	1-909-699-1771

Index